Liam Blackwood

The Passive Income Playbook: Proven Strategies to Build Wealth and Financial Freedom

TABLE OF CONTENTS

1. Introduction to Passive Income

1. Definition of passive income
2. Examples of passive income streams
3. Importance of passive income for financial freedom
4. Mindset shifts required for success
5. Overcoming common misconceptions about passive income
6. Developing a passive income mindset
7. Prioritizing passive income over active income
8. Balancing passive income with active income
9. Passive income as a path to financial independence
10. The power of compounding passive income

2. Evaluating Your Current Financial Situation

1. Tracking your income and expenses
2. Identifying areas for cost savings
3. Calculating your net worth
4. Assessing your risk tolerance
5. Determining your financial goals and timeline
6. Prioritizing financial goals
7. Creating a budget and sticking to it
8. Reducing debt and improving your credit score
9. Automating savings and investments
10. Reviewing and adjusting your financial plan regularly

3. Investing in Real Estate

1. Understanding the basics of real estate investing
2. Analyzing potential rental properties
3. Calculating cash flow and return on investment

4. Financing options for real estate investments
5. Strategies for finding and evaluating properties
6. Managing rental properties and tenants
7. Dealing with maintenance and repairs
8. Diversifying your real estate portfolio
9. Leveraging real estate to build wealth
10. Scaling your real estate investing business

4. Dividend Investing

1. Introduction to dividend investing
2. Understanding dividend yield and growth
3. Selecting high-quality dividend-paying stocks
4. Diversifying your dividend portfolio
5. Reinvesting dividends for compounding growth
6. Analyzing financial statements and company fundamentals
7. Identifying undervalued dividend stocks
8. Managing risk in dividend investing

9. Generating passive income through dividends
10. Dividend investing as a long-term wealth-building strategy

5. Affiliate Marketing

1. Understanding the basics of affiliate marketing
2. Choosing profitable affiliate programs
3. Creating valuable content and driving traffic
4. Optimizing your affiliate marketing strategy
5. Building an email list and nurturing leads
6. Leveraging social media for affiliate marketing
7. Tracking and analyzing your affiliate marketing performance
8. Scaling your affiliate marketing business
9. Avoiding common affiliate marketing pitfalls
10. Ethical considerations in affiliate marketing

6. Creating and Selling Digital Products

1. Identifying profitable digital product ideas
2. Conducting market research and validating your ideas
3. Creating valuable content and products
4. Choosing the right platform for selling digital products
5. Pricing your digital products effectively
6. Promoting and marketing your digital products
7. Building an email list and nurturing subscribers
8. Leveraging social media and influencer marketing
9. Automating the sales process for passive income
10. Continuously improving and updating your digital products

7. Investing in Stocks and ETFs

1. Understanding the basics of stock and ETF investing

2. Developing a long-term investment strategy
3. Diversifying your stock and ETF portfolio
4. Analyzing financial statements and company fundamentals
5. Identifying undervalued stocks and ETFs
6. Dollar-cost averaging and regular investing
7. Minimizing investment fees and taxes
8. Rebalancing your portfolio regularly
9. Investing in index funds and ETFs for passive income
10. Monitoring and adjusting your stock and ETF investments

8. Peer-to-Peer Lending

1. Understanding the basics of peer-to-peer lending
2. Evaluating lending platforms and their track records
3. Assessing borrower creditworthiness and risk
4. Diversifying your peer-to-peer lending portfolio

5. Calculating potential returns and risks
6. Automating your lending process for passive income
7. Monitoring and managing your peer-to-peer lending investments
8. Dealing with late payments and defaults
9. Reinvesting returns for compounding growth
10. Peer-to-peer lending as a fixed-income investment strategy

9. Automating and Scaling Your Passive Income

1. Leveraging technology to automate income streams
2. Outsourcing and delegating tasks to virtual assistants
3. Scaling your passive income business through partnerships
4. Automating content creation and marketing
5. Using email marketing and automation for passive income

6. Leveraging social media and influencer marketing
7. Optimizing your passive income streams for maximum returns
8. Diversifying your passive income sources
9. Scaling your passive income business while maintaining quality
10. Continuously learning and adapting to new opportunities

10. Maintaining and Optimizing Your Passive Income

1. Monitoring and analyzing your passive income streams
2. Identifying areas for improvement and optimization
3. Reinvesting profits and compounding wealth
4. Maintaining a long-term perspective and staying disciplined
5. Dealing with setbacks and challenges in passive income

6. Continuously learning and improving your skills
7. Balancing passive income with personal and professional goals
8. Achieving financial independence and freedom
9. Giving back and using passive income for good
10. Inspiring others and sharing your passive income journey

Chapter 1. Introduction to Passive Income

In today's fast-paced world, where the traditional 9-to-5 job is no longer the only path to financial security, the concept of passive income has gained significant traction. Passive income refers to the ability to generate consistent revenue streams with minimal ongoing effort, allowing you to achieve greater financial freedom and independence.

1. Definition of Passive Income

Passive income can be defined as money earned from sources other than traditional employment. This includes income from investments, rental properties, royalties, dividends, and various online business models. Unlike active income, which requires your direct time and effort, passive income streams continue to generate returns even when you're not actively working.Passive income is a type of unearned income that is acquired with little to no labor to earn or maintain. It is often combined with another source of income, such as regular employment or a side job. Passive income, as an acquired income, is taxable.

2. Examples of Passive Income Streams

Some common examples of passive income streams include:

- Rental income from real estate investments
- Dividends and interest from stocks, bonds, and other investments
- Royalties from creative works such as books, music, or patents
- Affiliate marketing commissions from promoting other companies' products or services
- Income from online businesses such as e-commerce stores, blogs, or online courses

One type of passive income is earnings from investments, like an Airbnb rental property, dividends, interest on savings, or leasing a piece of equipment that you own. Passive income can also be ongoing earnings from something you've previously created, such as sales revenue from a digital product like a prerecorded online course, or commission produced by affiliate marketing content.

3. Importance of Passive Income for Financial Freedom

The primary benefit of passive income is the ability to achieve financial freedom and independence. By diversifying your income sources beyond a single job, you can reduce your reliance on a regular paycheck and create a more stable and secure financial future. Passive income can also provide you with the flexibility to pursue your passions, spend more time with your family, or retire earlier.Passive income can be a great way to generate extra cash flow and build financial security. It can be a way of creating financial independence and early retirement, because the beneficiary will receive an income regardless of whether they are materially active in the activity creating the revenue.

4. Mindset Shifts Required for Success

Achieving success with passive income requires a fundamental shift in mindset. Instead of focusing solely on trading your time for money, you'll need to adopt a wealth-building mentality that prioritizes long-term financial growth over short-term gratification. This may involve delaying immediate gratification, investing in assets that generate passive income, and continuously learning and adapting to new opportunities.

5. Overcoming Common Misconceptions about Passive Income

Many people have misconceptions about passive income, believing it to be a get-rich-quick scheme or an easy path to wealth. In reality, building sustainable passive income streams requires dedication, patience, and a willingness to learn and adapt. It's important to understand that passive income is not entirely passive – it still requires an initial investment of time, effort, and resources to set up and maintain.Financial coach Todd Tresidder clarifies that passive income is not about getting something for nothing. It still requires work, but the labor is often front-loaded. You may need to put in effort upfront to create a product or maintain a rental property, but the ongoing income can provide financial security.

6. Developing a Passive Income Mindset

To succeed in building passive income, you'll need to cultivate a mindset that embraces the long-term approach. This may involve setting clear financial goals, developing a plan to achieve them, and consistently taking action to make progress. It's also crucial to stay motivated, overcome obstacles, and continuously learn and improve your strategies.

7. Prioritizing Passive Income over Active Income

While active income from traditional employment is essential for meeting your immediate financial needs, prioritizing passive income can help you achieve long-term financial security and independence. By investing in assets that generate passive income, you can create a foundation for wealth that continues to grow even when you're not actively working.

8. Balancing Passive Income with Active Income

It's important to strike a balance between passive income and active income. While passive income can provide you with financial freedom and flexibility, active income from traditional employment can still be valuable for providing stability, benefits, and opportunities for growth.

The key is to find a balance that works for your unique circumstances and goals.

9. Passive Income as a Path to Financial Independence

Passive income can be a powerful tool for achieving financial independence. By building multiple streams of passive income, you can create a safety net that protects you from the ups and downs of the job market and provides you with the resources to pursue your dreams. Financial independence can also give you the freedom to retire earlier or pursue more fulfilling work.

10. The Power of Compounding Passive Income

One of the most powerful aspects of passive income is the ability to compound your returns over time. By reinvesting your passive income into new assets or opportunities, you can accelerate your wealth-building efforts and create a snowball effect that continues to grow exponentially. The power of compounding can help you achieve your financial goals faster and with greater certainty.By understanding the fundamentals of passive income and adopting the right mindset, you'll be well on your way to creating a more secure and fulfilling financial future. In the following chapters, we'll dive deeper into specific strategies and techniques for building sustainable passive income streams.

Chapter 2. Evaluating Your Current Financial Situation

Evaluating your current financial situation is a critical step in understanding your financial health and setting the stage for achieving your financial goals. This chapter delves into a detailed analysis of various aspects of your finances to provide a comprehensive overview of your financial standing.

1. Assessing Income and Expenses

Begin by tracking your sources of income and expenses to gain a clear understanding of your cash flow. Analyze your income streams, including wages, investments, and other sources of revenue. Simultaneously, scrutinize your expenses, categorizing them into fixed expenses like rent and utilities, and variable expenses such as entertainment and dining out. This assessment helps you identify areas for potential cost savings and optimization.

2. Calculating Net Worth

Calculate your net worth by subtracting your liabilities from your assets. This calculation provides a snapshot of your overall financial position, indicating whether you have more assets than liabilities. Understanding your net worth is crucial for assessing your financial health and progress towards your financial goals.

3. Reviewing Debt Levels

Evaluate your current debt levels, including credit card debt, loans, and mortgages. Understanding your debt obligations is essential for managing your financial responsibilities and planning for debt repayment strategies. Assessing your debt-to-income ratio helps gauge your financial leverage and ability to take on additional financial commitments.

4. Analyzing Asset Distribution

Examine how your assets are distributed among different categories, such as liquid assets, real estate, personal possessions, and investment assets. Understanding the composition of your assets helps you assess your financial flexibility, emergency preparedness, and progress towards achieving specific financial objectives.

5. Assessing Risk Tolerance

Determine your risk tolerance level based on your financial goals, age, income, and investment experience. Your risk tolerance influences your investment decisions and asset allocation strategies. Aligning your risk tolerance with your financial goals ensures that your investment portfolio is tailored to your unique circumstances and aspirations.

6. Setting Financial Goals and Timeline

Define your short-term and long-term financial goals, such as saving for retirement, purchasing a home, or funding your children's education. Establishing clear financial objectives and timelines provides a roadmap for your financial journey and guides your investment decisions towards achieving these goals.

7. Creating a Budget and Sticking to It

Develop a comprehensive budget that aligns with your financial goals and priorities. A well-defined budget helps you track your spending, control expenses, and allocate resources towards savings and investments consistently. Adhering to your budget ensures financial discipline and progress towards your financial objectives.

8. Enhancing Tax Efficiency

Assess the tax efficiency of your investments and financial decisions to optimize after-tax returns. Consider tax-sheltered accounts for interest-generating assets and strategic structuring of loans to maximize tax deductions. Enhancing tax efficiency helps you retain more of your investment returns and manage tax liabilities effectively.

9. Safeguarding Assets

Identify assets that are vulnerable to loss, theft, or damage, and evaluate the need for insurance coverage to protect these assets. Ensuring adequate asset protection safeguards your financial well-being and mitigates potential risks that could impact your financial stability.

10. Regularly Reviewing and Adjusting Your Financial Plan

Continuously review and adjust your financial plan to reflect changes in your financial situation, goals, and market conditions. Regular monitoring allows you to stay on track towards your objectives, make informed decisions, and adapt your strategies to align with evolving circumstances.By meticulously evaluating your current financial situation across these key dimensions, you can gain a comprehensive understanding of your financial health, identify areas for improvement, and lay a solid foundation for achieving your financial aspirations. This detailed assessment serves as a cornerstone for effective financial planning and wealth management.

Chapter 3. Investing in Real Estate

Investing in real estate can be a lucrative strategy for building wealth and generating passive income. This chapter explores the fundamentals of real estate investing and provides insights into key considerations for successful property investment.

1. Understanding the Basics of Real Estate Investing

Begin by grasping the fundamental principles of real estate investing, including property appreciation, rental income, leverage, and tax benefits. Understanding these basics forms the foundation for making informed investment decisions in the real estate market.Real estate investing involves acquiring, owning, managing, and selling real estate properties for the purpose of generating income or capital appreciation. The two main types of real estate investments are residential properties, such as single-family homes, apartments, and condos, and commercial properties, such as office buildings, retail spaces, and industrial facilities.Real estate investors can generate income through rental payments from tenants and benefit from property appreciation over time. Leverage, which involves using borrowed capital to finance the purchase of an investment property, can amplify returns but also carries additional risk.

2. Analyzing Potential Rental Properties

Conduct thorough research and analysis to evaluate potential rental properties. Consider factors such as location, property condition, rental demand, and market trends to assess the investment potential of each property accurately.When analyzing potential rental properties, it's crucial to consider factors such as the property's age, condition, and any necessary repairs or renovations. The location of the property is also a key factor, as it can impact rental demand, property values, and the types of tenants attracted to the area.Conducting a comparative market analysis, which involves comparing the subject property to recently sold properties with similar characteristics, can help determine the property's fair market value and potential rental income.

3. Calculating Cash Flow and Return on Investment

Calculate the cash flow and return on investment (ROI) for prospective rental properties. Analyze rental income, operating expenses, financing costs, and potential appreciation to determine the profitability and financial viability of the investment.Cash flow is the net income generated by a rental property after all expenses have been paid, including mortgage payments, property taxes, insurance, and maintenance costs. Calculating cash flow helps investors determine the property's ability to generate positive returns.ROI measures the profitability of an investment relative to its cost. To calculate ROI, divide the net income generated by the property by the total investment amount, including the down payment and closing costs.

4. Financing Options for Real Estate Investments

Explore various financing options for real estate investments, including traditional mortgages, private lenders, and creative financing strategies. Assess the terms, interest rates, and repayment structures to select the most suitable financing option for your investment goals.Financing options for real estate investments include conventional mortgages, FHA loans, VA loans, hard money loans, and private money loans. Each financing option has its own requirements, terms, and interest rates, so it's important to compare and evaluate the options to find the best fit for your investment goals and financial situation.Creative financing strategies, such as lease options, seller financing, and real estate crowdfunding, can provide alternative paths to acquiring investment properties with less capital or more favorable terms.

5. Strategies for Finding and Evaluating Properties

Develop effective strategies for identifying and evaluating investment properties. Utilize online listings, real estate agents, networking, and market research to discover opportunities that align with your investment criteria and financial objectives.Strategies for finding investment properties include searching online listings, working with real estate agents, attending real estate investment club meetings, and networking with other investors. Once a potential property is identified, it's important to conduct a thorough evaluation, including a physical inspection, market analysis, and financial projections.Utilizing real estate investment software and online tools can help streamline the property evaluation process and analyze key metrics such as cash flow, ROI, and cap rates.

6. Managing Rental Properties and Tenants

Implement sound property management practices to effectively oversee rental properties and tenants. Establish clear lease agreements, conduct regular property inspections, address maintenance issues promptly, and cultivate positive tenant relationships to ensure smooth operations and maximize rental income.Effective property management is essential for generating consistent rental income and maintaining the value of the investment property. This includes screening tenants, collecting rent, handling maintenance and repairs, and addressing any tenant issues or concerns.Hiring a professional property management company can be beneficial for investors who lack the time, expertise, or desire to manage properties directly. However, it's important to carefully evaluate potential property management companies and their fees.

7. Dealing with Maintenance and Repairs

Prepare for maintenance and repair responsibilities associated with owning rental properties. Develop a proactive maintenance plan, budget for ongoing upkeep, and promptly address maintenance issues to preserve property value and tenant satisfaction.Regular maintenance and prompt repairs are crucial for maintaining the condition of the property and keeping tenants satisfied. Investors should budget for ongoing maintenance costs, such as landscaping, cleaning, and minor repairs, as well as set aside funds for unexpected repairs or major renovations.Establishing relationships with reliable contractors and tradespeople can help streamline the maintenance and repair process and ensure that issues are addressed efficiently and cost-effectively.

8. Diversifying Your Real Estate Portfolio

Consider diversifying your real estate portfolio by investing in different types of properties, locations, and investment strategies. Diversification helps mitigate risk, enhance returns, and create a balanced investment portfolio that aligns with your risk tolerance and financial goals.Diversifying a real estate portfolio can involve investing in different property types (e.g., single-family homes, multifamily properties, commercial buildings), different locations (e.g., urban, suburban, rural areas), and different investment strategies (e.g., fix-and-flip, buy-and-hold, real estate investment trusts).Diversification can help reduce the impact of localized market fluctuations and mitigate the risks associated with overexposure to a single property type or investment strategy.

9. Leveraging Real Estate to Build Wealth

Harness the power of real estate to build long-term wealth and financial security. Capitalize on property appreciation, rental income, tax advantages, and leverage to grow your real estate portfolio and create a sustainable source of passive income.Real estate investing offers several advantages for building wealth, including the potential for property appreciation, the ability to generate rental income, tax benefits such as deductions for mortgage interest and depreciation, and the use of leverage to acquire properties with a relatively small down payment.By reinvesting profits from rental income and property appreciation, investors can gradually expand their real estate portfolio and create a compounding effect on their wealth.

10. Scaling Your Real Estate Investing Business

Explore opportunities to scale your real estate investing business by expanding your property portfolio, leveraging partnerships, and implementing efficient property management systems. Scaling your real estate investments allows you to increase cash flow, diversify risk, and achieve greater financial success in the real estate market.Scaling a real estate investing business involves acquiring additional properties, leveraging partnerships with other investors or property management companies, and implementing systems and processes to streamline operations and maximize efficiency. As the portfolio grows, investors can benefit from economies of scale and increased cash flow, which can be reinvested to further expand the business.Seeking guidance from experienced real estate investors, attending industry events and conferences, and continuously educating oneself about market trends and best practices can help facilitate the scaling process and ensure long-term success in the real estate investing arena.By mastering the intricacies of real estate investing and implementing strategic approaches to property acquisition and management, you can unlock the potential of real estate as a wealth-building asset class and a cornerstone of your investment portfolio. This chapter serves as a comprehensive guide to navigating the real estate market and maximizing the returns on your real estate investments.

Additional Considerations

- **Real Estate Market Cycles**: Understand the real estate market cycles and how they impact property values and rental income.

- **Economic Indicators**: Monitor economic indicators such as GDP, inflation, and interest rates to anticipate market trends and adjust your investment strategy accordingly.

- **Local Market Conditions**: Research local market conditions, including population growth, job market trends, and infrastructure development, to identify areas with high potential for appreciation and rental income.

- **Property Management Software**: Utilize property management software to streamline operations, track financial performance, and optimize rental income.

- **Tax Strategies**: Implement tax strategies such as depreciation, interest deductions, and 1031 exchanges to minimize tax liabilities and maximize returns.

- **Risk Management**: Develop a risk management plan to mitigate potential risks such as tenant vacancies, property damage, and market fluctuations.

By considering these additional factors and implementing a comprehensive investment strategy, you can maximize the returns on your real estate investments and achieve long-term financial success.

Chapter 4. Dividend Investing

Dividend investing is a time-tested strategy that offers investors the opportunity to generate passive income and build long-term wealth through the consistent distribution of profits by companies. This chapter delves into the intricacies of dividend investing, providing a comprehensive guide to navigating the world of dividend-paying stocks.

1. Introduction to Dividend Investing

Dividend investing revolves around the concept of investing in companies that distribute a portion of their earnings to shareholders in the form of dividends. These regular cash payments serve as a source of passive income for investors, offering a steady stream of returns in addition to potential capital appreciation. Dividend-paying stocks have historically outperformed non-dividend-paying stocks over the long term, making them an attractive option for investors seeking both income and growth.Dividends provide a tangible return on investment, as investors receive a direct cash payment for their ownership stake in a company. This income can be particularly valuable in periods of market volatility or economic uncertainty, as it offers a cushion against potential losses. Furthermore, companies that pay dividends often exhibit strong financial health and stability, as they have the resources to distribute profits to shareholders while still investing in future growth.

2. Understanding Dividend Yield and Growth

Dividend yield is a key metric that measures the annual dividend income relative to the stock price, providing insight into the return on investment. A higher dividend yield generally indicates a more attractive investment opportunity, but it's important to consider the sustainability and growth potential of the dividend. Dividend growth signifies the rate at which a company increases its dividend payouts over time, reflecting financial health, stability, and a commitment to shareholder value.Investing in companies with a history of consistent dividend growth can provide a hedge against inflation and contribute to long-term wealth creation. High-yield stocks may offer attractive current income, but they may also carry higher risk if the dividend is not sustainable. Conversely, companies with a track record of dividend growth demonstrate their ability to generate consistent cash flow and allocate capital effectively, making them attractive long-term investments.

3. Selecting High-Quality Dividend-Paying Stocks

Choosing high-quality dividend-paying stocks involves evaluating companies with a history of consistent dividend payments, strong financial performance, and sustainable business models. Factors such as dividend payout ratio, earnings growth, and dividend sustainability are crucial considerations in the selection process. Investors should also look for companies with a competitive advantage, a strong management team, and the ability to generate consistent cash flow to support dividend payments. One key aspect of selecting high-quality dividend stocks is assessing the company's dividend payout ratio, which measures the percentage of earnings paid out as dividends. A payout ratio that is too high (above 100%) may indicate that the dividend is unsustainable, while a ratio that is too low (below 50%) may suggest that the company is retaining too much of its earnings and not returning enough value to shareholders. Investors should also consider the company's growth prospects and the potential for future dividend increases, as these factors can contribute to long-term returns.

4. Diversifying Your Dividend Portfolio

Diversification is essential in dividend investing to spread risk across various sectors and industries. By diversifying your dividend portfolio, you can minimize exposure to sector-specific risks and market volatility, enhancing the stability and resilience of your investment portfolio. A well-diversified dividend portfolio should include a mix of high-yield and dividend growth stocks, as well as a range of sectors and industries to mitigate concentration risk.Diversification is particularly important in dividend investing because certain sectors, such as utilities and consumer staples, tend to have higher dividend yields but lower growth potential, while other sectors, such as technology and healthcare, may have lower yields but higher growth prospects. By investing in a mix of these sectors, investors can balance their portfolio's income and growth potential. Additionally, diversifying across different company sizes, from large-cap blue chips to small-cap dividend growers, can provide exposure to various stages of the business cycle and growth trajectories.

5. Reinvesting Dividends for Compounding Growth

Reinvesting dividends through a dividend reinvestment plan (DRIP) can accelerate the growth of your investment portfolio through compounding. By reinvesting dividends to purchase additional shares, investors can benefit from the compounding effect, leading to exponential growth over time. Reinvesting dividends can significantly increase the long-term value of your portfolio, as the additional shares purchased will also generate dividends, creating a snowball effect. The power of compounding is particularly evident in dividend investing, as the reinvested dividends generate additional dividends, which can then be reinvested to purchase even more shares. Over time, this cycle can lead to substantial wealth accumulation, as the portfolio grows exponentially. Investors who reinvest their dividends consistently and for the long term can potentially double or triple their investment over a period of 10 to 20 years, depending on the dividend yield and growth rate of the underlying stocks.

6. Analyzing Financial Statements and Company Fundamentals

Thorough analysis of a company's financial statements and fundamentals is crucial in identifying high-quality dividend-paying stocks. Key metrics such as revenue growth, earnings per share, debt levels, and cash flow can provide valuable insights into the financial health and stability of a company. Investors should also assess a company's competitive position, market share, and growth prospects to determine its ability to sustain and grow its dividend payments over time.One important aspect of analyzing a company's financial statements is assessing its free cash flow, which represents the cash available for distribution to shareholders after accounting for capital expenditures and other operational expenses. A company with strong and consistent free cash flow is more likely to have the resources to maintain and grow its dividend payments. Investors should also look for companies with low debt levels and a history of prudent financial management, as these factors can contribute to the sustainability of the dividend.

7. Identifying Undervalued Dividend Stocks

Identifying undervalued dividend stocks presents an opportunity for investors to capitalize on potential growth and income. By conducting fundamental analysis and utilizing valuation metrics, such as price-to-earnings ratio and dividend yield, investors can uncover stocks trading below their intrinsic value. Investing in undervalued dividend stocks can provide a margin of safety and the potential for capital appreciation in addition to dividend income.One effective strategy for identifying undervalued dividend stocks is to look for companies that have experienced temporary setbacks or are operating in cyclical industries. These companies may be trading at a discount to their long-term intrinsic value, presenting an opportunity for investors to buy at a favorable price. Investors should also consider the company's growth prospects and the potential for future dividend increases, as these factors can contribute to long-term returns.

8. Managing Risk in Dividend Investing

Risk management is paramount in dividend investing to safeguard against potential pitfalls and market fluctuations. Strategies such as diversification, thorough research, and regular monitoring can help mitigate risks associated with individual stocks, sector-specific challenges, and broader market conditions. Investors should also be aware of the risks associated with high-yield stocks, as companies with unsustainably high dividend yields may be at risk of cutting or suspending their dividends.One key risk to consider in dividend investing is the potential for dividend cuts or suspensions, particularly during economic downturns or periods of industry-specific challenges. To mitigate this risk, investors should focus on companies with strong balance sheets, consistent cash flow, and a history of maintaining dividends through various market conditions. Regular monitoring of the companies in your portfolio and staying informed about industry trends and economic conditions can also help identify potential risks and opportunities.

9. Generating Passive Income through Dividends

Dividend investing offers a reliable source of passive income, allowing investors to receive regular cash payments without active involvement. By building a diversified portfolio of dividend-paying stocks, investors can create a steady income stream that can supplement other sources of revenue or serve as a primary income source. Dividend income can be used for living expenses, reinvestment, or other financial goals, providing flexibility and financial security.One advantage of generating passive income through dividends is that it can provide a cushion against market volatility. While the value of the underlying stocks may fluctuate, the dividend payments can provide a stable source of income that is less affected by short-term market movements. This can be particularly valuable for investors who are retired or nearing retirement and are seeking a reliable stream of income to fund their lifestyle.

10. Dividend Investing as a Long-Term Wealth-Building Strategy

Dividend investing is not just about immediate income but also serves as a long-term wealth-building strategy. By consistently reinvesting dividends, investors can harness the power of compounding to grow their investment portfolio over time, leading to substantial wealth accumulation and financial security in the future. The combination of dividend income and capital appreciation can provide a strong foundation for building long-term wealth, making dividend investing a compelling option for investors with a long-term investment horizon.One of the key advantages of dividend investing as a long-term wealth-building strategy is its ability to provide a hedge against inflation. As companies increase their dividend payments over time, the real value of the income stream is maintained, even as the purchasing power of the dollar declines. This can help preserve the purchasing power of the investment portfolio and ensure that the investor's financial goals are met over the long term.By mastering the nuances of dividend investing and adhering to a disciplined investment approach, investors can leverage the benefits of dividend-paying stocks to achieve their financial objectives and secure a prosperous financial future.

Chapter 5. Affiliate Marketing

Affiliate marketing is a popular online business model that allows individuals to earn commissions by promoting products or services offered by other companies. This chapter explores the intricacies of affiliate marketing, providing insights into key strategies and considerations for success in this dynamic industry.

1. Understanding the Basics of Affiliate Marketing

Affiliate marketing involves promoting products or services through unique affiliate links and earning a commission for each sale or lead generated. It is a performance-based marketing strategy that benefits both the affiliate marketer and the merchant, as affiliates can earn passive income while companies can expand their reach and boost sales. The affiliate marketer is responsible for driving traffic and conversions to the merchant's offers, while the merchant provides the products or services and tracks the performance of the affiliate's promotional efforts.The affiliate marketing industry has grown significantly in recent years, with global spending on affiliate marketing expected to reach $8.2 billion by 2022.

This growth can be attributed to the increasing popularity of online shopping, the rise of influencer marketing, and the ability of affiliate marketing to provide a measurable return on investment for both merchants and affiliates. To succeed in affiliate marketing, it is essential to understand the various roles and responsibilities involved. Merchants, also known as advertisers, are the companies that offer products or services and provide affiliate programs for individuals to promote their offerings. Affiliates, also known as publishers, are the individuals or entities that promote the merchant's products or services through their own channels, such as websites, blogs, social media platforms, or email lists. Affiliate networks serve as intermediaries between merchants and affiliates, providing a platform for managing affiliate programs, tracking performance, and facilitating payments.

2. Choosing Profitable Affiliate Programs

Selecting the right affiliate programs is crucial for success in affiliate marketing. Consider factors such as product relevance, commission rates, cookie duration, and the reputation of the merchant. Choose programs that align with your niche and target audience to maximize your earning potential. Relevance is key, as promoting products or services that are closely related to your content and audience interests will increase the likelihood of conversions and repeat business.Commission rates vary widely across different affiliate programs, with some offering a percentage of the sale price while others provide a fixed amount per sale or lead. Cookie duration refers to the length of time a merchant's cookie remains active on a visitor's browser after clicking an affiliate link. Longer cookie durations increase the chances of a conversion being attributed to the affiliate, even if the purchase occurs at a later date. It is also essential to consider the merchant's reputation, as promoting products or services from reputable and trustworthy companies can enhance your credibility and increase customer trust.When evaluating potential affiliate programs, it is important to conduct thorough research and compare the terms and conditions of different offers. Look for programs that provide clear and transparent information about their commission structure, cookie duration, and payment terms. Consider the merchant's track record of paying affiliates on time and honoring their commitments. Joining reputable affiliate networks can provide access to a wide range of high-quality affiliate programs and offer additional support and resources for affiliates.

3. Creating Valuable Content and Driving Traffic

Content creation is key to a successful affiliate marketing strategy. Develop high-quality, engaging content that provides value to your audience and incorporates affiliate links naturally. Utilize SEO techniques, social media promotion, and email marketing to drive traffic to your affiliate offers and increase conversions. Creating valuable content is essential for building trust with your audience and establishing yourself as an authority in your niche.When creating content, focus on providing informative, entertaining, or educational material that addresses the needs and interests of your target audience. Product reviews, tutorials, and how-to guides are popular types of content that can effectively showcase affiliate products while providing value to readers. Ensure that your content is well-researched, well-written, and visually appealing to engage your audience and encourage them to click on your affiliate links.Optimizing your content for search engines is crucial for driving organic traffic to your affiliate offers. Conduct keyword research to identify relevant search terms that your target audience is using, and incorporate these keywords naturally into your content. Use meta tags, alt text, and internal linking to improve your website's SEO and make it easier for search engines to find and rank your content. Additionally, promote your content through social media platforms and email marketing campaigns to reach a wider audience and drive more traffic to your affiliate offers.

4. Optimizing Your Affiliate Marketing Strategy

Continuously optimize your affiliate marketing strategy by testing different promotional methods, tracking performance metrics, and refining your approach based on data-driven insights. Experiment with various tactics, such as A/B testing, landing page optimization, and audience segmentation, to enhance your results. Optimization is an ongoing process that requires constant monitoring, analysis, and adjustment to achieve the best possible outcomes.A/B testing involves creating two versions of a piece of content or promotional material and comparing their performance to determine which one is more effective. This could include testing different headlines, images, calls-to-action, or placement of affiliate links. By analyzing the results of your A/B tests, you can make data-driven decisions about which elements to keep or change in your affiliate marketing strategy.Landing page optimization involves improving the effectiveness of the pages where visitors land after clicking on your affiliate links. Ensure that your landing pages are visually appealing, easy to navigate, and clearly communicate the benefits of the product or service being promoted. Use persuasive copywriting, social proof, and clear calls-to-action to encourage visitors to take the desired action, such as making a purchase or filling out a lead form.Audience segmentation involves dividing your audience into smaller, more targeted groups based on factors such as demographics, interests, or behavior. By tailoring your content and promotional efforts to specific segments of your audience, you can increase the relevance and effectiveness of your affiliate marketing strategy. For example, you might create different content or offers for new visitors versus returning visitors, or for subscribers versus non-subscribers.

5. Building an Email List and Nurturing Leads

Building an email list is a powerful way to cultivate relationships with your audience and promote affiliate offers effectively. Create valuable lead magnets, segment your email list based on interests, and provide personalized recommendations to drive conversions and build long-term customer loyalty. Email marketing allows you to stay in touch with your audience, share valuable content, and promote affiliate offers in a more targeted and personalized manner.Lead magnets are free resources or incentives that you offer in exchange for an email address. Examples include ebooks, checklists, webinars, or exclusive discounts. By providing value upfront, you can attract potential customers and build your email list. Segment your email list based on factors such as lead magnet downloaded, purchase history, or engagement level. This allows you to send more targeted and relevant emails to each segment, increasing the likelihood of conversions.Nurturing your email leads is crucial for building trust and loyalty over time. Send a series of welcome emails introducing yourself and your brand, and then continue to provide valuable content and offers on a regular basis. Personalize your emails with the recipient's name and tailor the content to their interests and needs. Promote affiliate offers in a natural and non-intrusive way, focusing on the benefits to the reader rather than just the commission you'll earn. By consistently providing value and building relationships with your email subscribers, you can increase the effectiveness of your affiliate marketing efforts and generate more sales over the long term.

6. Leveraging Social Media for Affiliate Marketing

Social media platforms offer a valuable opportunity to reach a wider audience and promote affiliate products authentically. Develop a social media strategy that aligns with your brand voice, engages your followers, and encourages interaction with your affiliate links to drive traffic and conversions. Social media can be a powerful tool for building relationships, sharing content, and driving sales for your affiliate marketing business.When leveraging social media for affiliate marketing, it's important to choose the platforms that are most relevant to your target audience and niche. Different platforms cater to different demographics and content types, so it's essential to focus your efforts on the ones that are most likely to yield results. For example, if you're promoting visual products like fashion or home decor, Instagram and Pinterest may be more effective than Twitter or LinkedIn.Engage with your followers by sharing valuable content, responding to comments, and participating in relevant conversations. Use relevant hashtags to increase the visibility of your posts and reach a wider audience. Collaborate with other influencers or brands in your niche to cross-promote content and expand your reach. When promoting affiliate offers, be transparent about your relationship with the merchant and focus on providing value to your followers rather than just making a sale.Measure the performance of your social media efforts by tracking metrics such as engagement rate, click-through rate, and conversion rate. Use this data to refine your strategy and optimize your content for better results. Experiment with different types of content, such as images, videos, polls, or live streams, to see what resonates best with your audience. By consistently engaging with your followers and providing value through social media, you can build trust, drive traffic to your affiliate offers, and generate more sales over time.

7. Tracking and Analyzing Your Affiliate Marketing Performance

Tracking and analyzing key performance metrics is essential for optimizing your affiliate marketing efforts. Monitor click-through rates, conversion rates, earnings per click, and other relevant data to identify trends, assess the effectiveness of your campaigns, and make informed decisions to improve your results. Accurate tracking and analysis allow you to allocate your resources more effectively, identify areas for improvement, and make data-driven decisions to enhance your affiliate marketing strategy. Click-through rate (CTR) measures the percentage of people who click on your affiliate links out of the total number of people who see them. A high CTR indicates that your content is engaging and relevant to your audience. Conversion rate measures the percentage of people who take the desired action, such as making a purchase or filling out a lead form, after clicking on your affiliate links. Earnings per click (EPC) is a metric that calculates the average amount of revenue generated per click on your affiliate links. Analyze these metrics at the campaign, channel, and product level to identify patterns and trends. For example, you might notice that certain types of content or promotional methods consistently generate higher CTRs or conversion rates than others. Use this information to replicate successful strategies and optimize underperforming areas. Monitor your earnings over time to identify any fluctuations or changes in your revenue stream. Many affiliate networks and merchants provide tracking tools and analytics dashboards to help affiliates monitor their performance. Utilize these tools to track your metrics and gain insights into your affiliate marketing efforts. Additionally, consider using third-party tracking solutions or custom tracking links to gain more granular data and control over your performance metrics.

8. Scaling Your Affiliate Marketing Business

Scaling your affiliate marketing business involves expanding your reach, diversifying your income streams, and increasing your earning potential. Explore new affiliate programs, collaborate with other affiliates or influencers, and consider outsourcing tasks to streamline your operations and grow your business. Scaling requires a strategic approach that balances growth with sustainability and profitability.One way to scale your affiliate marketing business is to diversify your income streams by promoting multiple affiliate programs across different niches or industries. This reduces your reliance on a single merchant or product and helps to mitigate risk. However, it's important to maintain relevance and authenticity when promoting a diverse range of products or services.Collaborating with other affiliates or influencers can also help you scale your business by tapping into new audiences and leveraging existing relationships. Consider guest posting on each other's blogs, co-creating content, or promoting each other's affiliate offers to mutual benefit. Ensure that any collaborations align with your brand values and target audience.Outsourcing tasks such as content creation, social media management, or email marketing can help you scale your business more efficiently by freeing up your time and resources. Hire freelancers or virtual assistants to handle specific tasks, allowing you to focus on high-level strategy and growth initiatives. However, it's important to maintain quality control and ensure that any outsourced work aligns with your brand voice and standards.

9. Avoiding Common Affiliate Marketing Pitfalls

Avoid common pitfalls in affiliate marketing by disclosing your affiliate relationships transparently, focusing on building trust with your audience, and avoiding spammy or unethical promotional tactics. Prioritize providing value to your audience and maintaining integrity in your marketing efforts to foster long-term success. Falling into common traps can damage your reputation, erode trust with your audience, and ultimately limit your earning potential.One common pitfall is failing to disclose affiliate relationships clearly and transparently. Many countries have regulations that require affiliates to disclose their relationships with merchants, and failure to do so can result in legal issues or penalties. Be upfront about your affiliate relationships in your content, social media posts, and any other promotional materials. Another pitfall is promoting products or services that are irrelevant, low-quality, or unethical. Prioritize promoting products that align with your brand values and provide genuine value to your audience. Avoid promoting products with a history of customer complaints, poor quality, or deceptive marketing practices. Building trust with your audience takes time and effort, but it's essential for long-term success in affiliate marketing. Spammy or intrusive promotional tactics, such as sending unsolicited emails, posting affiliate links on irrelevant forums or social media groups, or using misleading headlines or images, can also damage your reputation and limit your success. Focus on providing value through high-quality content and authentic promotions, rather than resorting to manipulative tactics.

10. Ethical Considerations in Affiliate Marketing

Maintaining ethical standards in affiliate marketing is essential for building credibility and trust with your audience. Disclose your affiliate relationships clearly, only promote products or services that align with your values and are beneficial to your audience, and prioritize transparency and authenticity in your marketing communications. Ethical affiliate marketing not only builds trust with your audience but also contributes to the long-term sustainability and growth of the industry as a whole. When disclosing affiliate relationships, be clear and upfront about the fact that you may earn a commission if someone clicks on your link and makes a purchase. Use language such as "affiliate link" or "commission" to indicate that you have a financial relationship with the merchant. Avoid hiding or burying your disclosures in fine print or at the bottom of your content. Promote products or services that you genuinely believe in and that provide value to your audience. Avoid promoting products that are low-quality, overpriced, or deceptive. If you have any doubts about the integrity or quality of a product, it's best to avoid promoting it altogether. Prioritize authenticity and transparency in your marketing communications, and avoid making exaggerated claims or promises about the products you promote. Maintain high standards of quality and consistency in your content and promotions. Avoid using spammy or manipulative tactics, such as sending unsolicited emails, posting affiliate links on irrelevant forums or social media groups, or using misleading headlines or images. Focus on providing value to your audience and building long-term relationships based on trust and mutual benefit.By adhering to ethical standards and prioritizing the needs of your audience, you can build a successful and sustainable affiliate marketing business that generates passive income while contributing positively to the industry as a whole.

Chapter 6. Creating and Selling Digital Products

In the digital age, creating and selling your own products can be a highly lucrative and scalable business model. This chapter explores the key strategies and considerations for identifying, developing, and successfully marketing digital products to generate passive income.

1. Identifying Profitable Digital Product Ideas

The first step in creating and selling digital products is to identify ideas that have the potential to be profitable. Consider your own expertise, interests, and the needs of your target audience. Look for pain points, problems, or desires that you can address through your digital products. Research popular topics, trends, and best-selling products in your niche to uncover opportunities.When evaluating potential digital product ideas, consider factors such as market demand, competition, pricing potential, and your ability to create and deliver the product effectively. Identify areas where you can provide unique value, differentiate your offerings, and meet the needs of your target customers. Analyze the competitive landscape to understand what similar products or solutions are already available and how you can position your offerings to stand out.One effective approach is to leverage your own experiences and expertise. Reflect on the challenges you've faced, the skills you've developed, and the knowledge you've acquired in your personal or professional life. These can serve as the foundation for creating valuable digital products that resonate with your target audience. Additionally, pay attention to the questions, concerns, and pain points that your existing customers or followers express, as these can provide valuable insights for developing new digital products.

2. Conducting Market Research and Validating Your Ideas

Before investing time and resources into creating a digital product, it's crucial to conduct thorough market research and validate your ideas. Engage with your target audience, gather feedback, and assess the viability of your product concepts. This can involve surveys, interviews, online forums, and competitor analysis to gauge interest, identify pain points, and understand pricing expectations.Validating your ideas through market research helps you make informed decisions, reduce the risk of creating a product that doesn't resonate with your audience, and ensure that you're investing your efforts in the most promising opportunities. This process can also provide valuable insights to guide the development and positioning of your digital products.When conducting market research, seek to understand the specific needs, pain points, and preferences of your target audience. Engage with them directly through surveys, interviews, or online communities to gather qualitative feedback on your product ideas. Analyze the language they use, the challenges they face, and the solutions they're seeking. This information can inform the development of your digital products, ensuring that they address the real needs of your customers.Additionally, research your competitors to understand their offerings, pricing, and marketing strategies. Identify gaps in the market that your digital products can fill, or ways in which you can differentiate your offerings to provide unique value. Analyze customer reviews and feedback for competing products to uncover opportunities for improvement or innovation.

3. Creating Valuable Content and Products

The foundation of a successful digital product is the creation of high-quality, valuable content and resources. Leverage your expertise, research, and creativity to develop content that addresses the specific needs and pain points of your target audience. This can include ebooks, online courses, video tutorials, templates, software applications, or any other digital asset that provides tangible value to your customers. When creating your digital products, focus on delivering exceptional quality, clarity, and usability. Ensure that your content is well-organized, easy to consume, and tailored to the learning preferences and requirements of your target audience. Invest time in refining your products, testing them with beta users, and incorporating feedback to continuously improve the user experience. One key aspect of creating valuable digital products is to deeply understand your target audience and their specific needs. Conduct user research, gather feedback, and continuously iterate on your products to ensure they align with the evolving requirements of your customers. Leverage multimedia formats, such as video, audio, and interactive elements, to enhance the learning experience and engagement. Additionally, consider creating a series of complementary digital products that build upon each other or address different aspects of your target audience's needs. This can create a cohesive ecosystem of offerings and foster long-term customer relationships. Continuously seek opportunities to expand your product line, cross-sell related products, and provide additional value to your customers.

4. Choosing the Right Platform for Selling Digital Products

Selecting the appropriate platform for selling your digital products is crucial for maximizing your reach, sales, and overall success. Consider factors such as the features, pricing, and target audience of various platforms, including your own website, online marketplaces (e.g., Amazon, Udemy), and specialized digital product platforms (e.g., Gumroad, Teachable).Each platform offers unique advantages and disadvantages, so it's essential to evaluate your specific needs, target audience, and the type of digital products you're offering. Factors such as branding, control over the sales process, and access to customer data can influence your platform selection.When choosing a platform, consider the level of customization and control you require over the sales process, the integration capabilities with your existing marketing and sales tools, and the potential for scalability as your business grows. Online marketplaces may provide broader reach and built-in credibility, but they often have less control over branding and customer data. Specialized digital product platforms may offer more features and customization options, but may have a smaller audience reach.It's also important to consider the fees and commission structures associated with different platforms, as these can significantly impact your profitability. Evaluate the platform's reputation, customer support, and the overall user experience to ensure a seamless selling process for both you and your customers.

5. Pricing Your Digital Products Effectively

Determining the right pricing for your digital products is a critical aspect of your business strategy. Consider factors such as production costs, market demand, competitor pricing, and the perceived value of your offerings. Experiment with different pricing models, such as one-time purchases, subscriptions, or tiered pricing, to find the sweet spot that balances profitability and customer perceived value.Effective pricing strategies can include offering introductory discounts, bundling products, or implementing dynamic pricing based on factors like seasonality or customer segmentation. Continuously monitor your pricing, gather customer feedback, and adjust as needed to optimize your revenue and profitability.When pricing your digital products, it's essential to strike a balance between perceived value and affordability. Research the pricing of similar products in your industry to understand the market range, but don't be afraid to price your offerings higher if you can demonstrate exceptional value. Factors such as the depth of content, the level of expertise, and the overall user experience can justify a premium price point.Additionally, consider offering different pricing tiers or product bundles to cater to the diverse needs and budgets of your target audience. This can include basic, standard, and premium versions of your digital products, or the ability to purchase individual modules or the entire product suite. Carefully analyze the perceived value and willingness to pay for each pricing tier to maximize your revenue potential.Regularly review and adjust your pricing based on customer feedback, sales data, and market trends. Be prepared to experiment with different pricing strategies and monitor the impact on your sales and profitability. Maintaining flexibility and responsiveness in your pricing approach can help you optimize your digital product offerings for long-term success.

6. Promoting and Marketing Your Digital Products

Promoting and marketing your digital products is essential for driving awareness, generating sales, and building a loyal customer base. Leverage a variety of marketing channels, such as search engine optimization (SEO), social media, email marketing, affiliate partnerships, and influencer collaborations, to reach your target audience effectively.Develop a comprehensive content marketing strategy that includes blog posts, videos, webinars, and social media content to educate and engage your audience. Utilize targeted advertising campaigns on platforms like Google, Facebook, or LinkedIn to reach potential customers and drive traffic to your digital product offerings.When promoting your digital products, focus on highlighting the unique value proposition, the specific benefits, and the transformation or outcome that your customers can expect. Craft compelling and persuasive messaging that resonates with your target audience and addresses their pain points or desires. Leverage social proof, such as customer testimonials or case studies, to build trust and credibility.Explore partnerships with relevant influencers, industry experts, or complementary businesses to cross-promote your digital products to new audiences. Collaborate on content creation, joint webinars, or affiliate marketing campaigns to leverage the reach and credibility of your partners.Continuously monitor the performance of your marketing efforts, analyze data, and refine your strategies based on what's working best. A/B testing, tracking key metrics, and making data-driven decisions can help you optimize your promotional activities and maximize the return on your marketing investments.

7. Building an Email List and Nurturing Subscribers

Building and nurturing an email list is a powerful way to establish long-term relationships with your customers and promote your digital products effectively. Offer valuable lead magnets, such as free ebooks or exclusive content, to incentivize email sign-ups. Segment your list based on customer behavior, interests, and purchase history to deliver personalized and relevant communications.Consistently provide your email subscribers with valuable content, updates, and exclusive offers to keep them engaged and interested in your digital products. Utilize email automation and drip campaigns to nurture leads, cross-sell related products, and encourage repeat purchases.When building your email list, focus on attracting the right subscribers – those who are genuinely interested in your products and offerings. Avoid the temptation of buying email lists or using questionable tactics to grow your list, as this can lead to low engagement, high unsubscribe rates, and potential deliverability issues.Segment your email list based on factors such as lead magnet downloaded, purchase history, or engagement level. This allows you to send more targeted and relevant communications, increasing the likelihood of conversions and repeat business. Experiment with different lead magnet offers, email subject lines, and content formats to optimize your email marketing strategy.Nurture your email subscribers by providing them with valuable, educational, and entertaining content on a consistent basis. This helps to build trust, establish your expertise, and keep your digital products top-of-mind. Leverage email automation to deliver a series of welcome emails, product updates, and personalized recommendations to your subscribers.

8. Leveraging Social Media and Influencer Marketing

Social media platforms offer a powerful avenue for promoting and selling your digital products. Develop a strong social media presence, create engaging content, and leverage the reach of influencers and industry experts to amplify your message and drive sales.Collaborate with relevant influencers or industry leaders to co-create content, host webinars, or promote your digital products to their engaged audiences. Leverage user-generated content and social proof to build trust and credibility with potential customers.When leveraging social media, focus on the platforms that are most relevant to your target audience and the type of digital products you're offering. Different social media channels cater to different demographics and content preferences, so it's essential to prioritize the platforms that are most likely to yield the best results.Develop a content strategy that aligns with your brand voice and resonates with your target audience. Share a mix of educational, entertaining, and promotional content to keep your followers engaged. Utilize features like live streams, video content, and interactive polls to increase engagement and foster a sense of community around your digital products.Collaborating with influencers or industry experts can help you tap into new audiences and leverage the trust and credibility that these individuals have built with their followers. Carefully vet potential influencer partners to ensure they align with your brand values and can authentically promote your digital products. Negotiate mutually beneficial partnerships, such as revenue sharing or co-creation opportunities, to maximize the impact of your influencer marketing efforts.

9. Automating the Sales Process for Passive Income

Automating the sales process for your digital products is key to generating passive income and scaling your business. Implement strategies such as automated email sequences, sales funnels, and self-service checkout to streamline the customer journey and minimize manual intervention.Leverage tools and platforms that integrate with your digital product offerings, allowing customers to purchase and access your products seamlessly. Automate the delivery of digital products, the management of customer accounts, and the processing of payments to create a hands-off, scalable sales process.When automating your sales process, focus on creating a frictionless customer experience. Ensure that the purchase and delivery of your digital products are seamless, with clear instructions and easy access for your customers. Implement secure payment gateways, automated email confirmations, and self-service account management to enhance the overall user experience.Utilize sales funnels and automated email sequences to guide potential customers through the buyer's journey, from initial awareness to conversion and beyond. Craft compelling and personalized email campaigns that nurture leads, cross-sell related products, and encourage repeat purchases. Leverage marketing automation tools to trigger these sequences based on customer actions, such as downloading a lead magnet or abandoning a shopping cart.Continuously monitor and optimize your automated sales processes to improve conversion rates, customer satisfaction, and overall profitability. Analyze data, gather customer feedback, and make iterative improvements to ensure that your sales automation strategies are aligned with the evolving needs and preferences of your target audience.

10. Continuously Improving and Updating Your Digital Products

Maintaining and improving your digital products is an ongoing process that ensures their continued relevance, value, and competitiveness in the market. Regularly gather customer feedback, monitor industry trends, and identify opportunities for product enhancements, updates, and new offerings.Implement a systematic approach to product development, including roadmapping, beta testing, and iterative improvements. Continuously refine your digital products based on customer needs, technological advancements, and market changes to maintain a competitive edge and foster long-term customer loyalty.When gathering customer feedback, utilize a variety of channels, such as surveys, reviews, and direct communication. Analyze the feedback to identify areas for improvement, new feature requests, and potential pain points that your customers are experiencing. Incorporate this feedback into your product roadmap and prioritize updates that will have the greatest impact on customer satisfaction and retention.Stay informed about industry trends, emerging technologies, and evolving customer preferences. Continuously research your competitors, monitor market shifts, and identify opportunities to differentiate your digital products. Leverage this knowledge to proactively update your offerings, introduce new products, and maintain a competitive advantage.Implement a structured product development process that includes planning, prototyping, testing, and iterative refinement. Engage with beta users or early adopters to gather feedback and validate your product enhancements before rolling them out to your entire customer base. This approach helps ensure that your digital products remain relevant, user-friendly, and aligned with the evolving needs of your target audience. By mastering the strategies and best practices outlined in this chapter, you can leverage the power of digital products to build a sustainable and scalable passive income stream, while providing immense value to your target audience.

Chapter 7. Investing in Stocks and ETFs

Investing in stocks and Exchange-Traded Funds (ETFs) can be a rewarding way to build wealth and achieve financial goals. This chapter delves into the fundamentals of stock and ETF investing, providing insights into key strategies and considerations for successful investment in the financial markets.

1. Understanding the Basics of Stock and ETF Investing

Stock investing involves purchasing shares of individual companies, representing ownership in the company and potential for capital appreciation and dividends. ETFs are investment funds that hold a diversified portfolio of assets, offering investors exposure to a range of securities within a single investment. Understanding the differences between stocks and ETFs, as well as the risks and rewards associated with each, is essential for building a well-rounded investment portfolio.When investing in stocks, you become a partial owner of the company, with the potential to benefit from its growth and profitability. Stocks can provide capital appreciation if the company's share price increases, as well as potential dividend income if the company pays dividends to its shareholders. However, investing in individual stocks also carries higher risk, as the performance of a single company can be more volatile and susceptible to company-specific risks, such as management changes, product failures, or industry disruptions.ETFs, on the other hand, offer instant diversification by holding a basket of securities that track a specific index, sector, or investment theme. ETFs provide exposure to a wide range of assets, including stocks, bonds, commodities, and real estate, all within a single investment vehicle. ETFs typically have lower fees compared to actively managed mutual funds and offer tax efficiency due to their passive management approach. Investing in ETFs can help reduce risk by spreading your investments across multiple securities and asset classes.Understanding the differences in risk and return profiles between stocks and ETFs is crucial for constructing a balanced investment portfolio. While individual stocks offer the potential for higher returns, they also carry higher risk. ETFs, on the other hand, provide diversification and lower risk, but may have lower potential returns compared to individual stocks. Combining both stocks and ETFs in your portfolio can help you achieve a balance between risk and return, while also providing exposure to various sectors and asset classes.

2. Developing a Long-Term Investment Strategy

Developing a long-term investment strategy is crucial for achieving financial goals and navigating market fluctuations. Define your investment objectives, risk tolerance, and time horizon to establish a clear roadmap for your investment journey. Consider factors such as asset allocation, diversification, and periodic review to ensure your investment strategy remains aligned with your financial objectives.When developing your long-term investment strategy, it's essential to start by clearly defining your financial goals. Are you saving for retirement, a down payment on a house, or your child's education? Knowing your specific goals will help you determine the appropriate investment time horizon and risk tolerance. For example, if you have a longer time horizon, such as retirement planning, you may be able to take on more risk in pursuit of higher returns. Conversely, if you have a shorter time horizon, such as saving for a down payment, you may want to adopt a more conservative approach to preserve capital.Asset allocation is another critical component of your long-term investment strategy.

Diversifying your investments across different asset classes, such as stocks, bonds, real estate, and cash, can help manage risk and enhance returns. The specific asset allocation will depend on your risk tolerance, time horizon, and investment objectives. As a general rule, investors with a longer time horizon and higher risk tolerance may allocate a larger portion of their portfolio to stocks, while those with a shorter time horizon and lower risk tolerance may favor bonds and cash.Regularly reviewing and adjusting your investment strategy is essential to ensure it remains aligned with your evolving financial goals and market conditions. As you approach your investment goals or experience significant life changes, such as marriage, children, or job changes, it's important to reassess your investment strategy and make necessary adjustments. Periodic portfolio rebalancing can help maintain your desired asset allocation and risk profile over time.

3. Diversifying Your Stock and ETF Portfolio

Diversification is a key principle in investing that involves spreading your investments across different asset classes, industries, and geographic regions to reduce risk and enhance returns. Build a diversified stock and ETF portfolio to mitigate the impact of market volatility and sector-specific risks, ensuring a balanced and resilient investment strategy.Diversification helps reduce the overall risk of your investment portfolio by ensuring that you are not overly exposed to any single security, industry, or market segment. When one investment or sector experiences losses, the impact on your overall portfolio can be minimized by the gains in other investments or sectors. This helps to smooth out the volatility of your returns and provides a cushion against market downturns.When diversifying your stock and ETF portfolio, consider investing in a range of industries and sectors to reduce concentration risk. Avoid over-allocating to any single sector or industry, as this can expose your portfolio to sector-specific risks. For example, if you have a significant portion of your portfolio invested in technology stocks, you may be vulnerable to the risks associated with that sector, such as rapid technological changes, intense competition, or regulatory challenges.Geographic diversification is another important aspect of portfolio diversification. Investing in international stocks and ETFs can provide exposure to different economic and political environments, reducing the impact of domestic market fluctuations on your portfolio. However, international investments also carry additional risks, such as currency fluctuations, political instability, and varying accounting standards, which should be carefully considered.Regularly reviewing and rebalancing your diversified portfolio is essential to maintain your desired risk profile and asset allocation. As market conditions change and some investments outperform others, your portfolio's asset allocation may drift from your original targets. Rebalancing involves selling some of the investments that have grown too large and using the proceeds to buy more of the investments that have become underweighted. This process helps to keep your portfolio aligned with your long-term investment strategy and risk tolerance.

4. Analyzing Financial Statements and Company Fundamentals

Analyzing financial statements and company fundamentals is essential for evaluating the performance and valuation of individual stocks and ETFs. Conduct thorough research on key metrics such as revenue growth, earnings per share, debt levels, and profit margins to assess the financial health and stability of companies in your investment portfolio. Utilize fundamental analysis to make informed investment decisions based on the intrinsic value of securities.Financial statements, such as the balance sheet, income statement, and cash flow statement, provide a wealth of information about a company's financial performance and health. By analyzing these statements, you can gain insights into a company's revenue growth, profitability, debt levels, and cash flow generation. This information can help you assess the company's ability to generate sustainable earnings, pay dividends, and withstand economic downturns.One of the most commonly used metrics in fundamental analysis is the price-to-earnings (P/E) ratio, which compares a company's stock price to its earnings per share. A low P/E ratio may indicate that a stock is undervalued, while a high P/E ratio may suggest that a stock is overvalued. However, it's important to consider the company's growth prospects, industry, and overall market conditions when interpreting the P/E ratio.Other key metrics to analyze include the debt-to-equity ratio, which measures a company's financial leverage, and the profit margin, which indicates the company's profitability. A company with low debt levels and high profit margins may be considered financially healthy and well-positioned for growth.When analyzing ETFs, focus on the underlying index or investment theme, the fund's expense ratio, and its historical performance compared to its benchmark. Look for ETFs with low expense ratios, a clear and consistent investment strategy, and a track record of outperforming their benchmarks over time.Fundamental analysis is an ongoing process that requires continuous monitoring of company and market developments. Stay informed about industry trends, economic conditions, and regulatory changes that may impact the companies and sectors in your investment portfolio. Regularly review and update your analysis to ensure that your investment decisions are based on the most current and accurate information.

5. Identifying Undervalued Stocks and ETFs

Identifying undervalued stocks and ETFs presents an opportunity for investors to capitalize on potential growth and income. Utilize valuation metrics such as price-to-earnings ratio, price-to-book ratio, and dividend yield to assess whether a stock or ETF is trading below its intrinsic value. Conduct in-depth research and analysis to uncover investment opportunities that offer favorable risk-reward profiles and long-term growth potential.Identifying undervalued stocks requires a combination of quantitative and qualitative analysis. Start by screening for stocks with low valuation ratios, such as price-to-earnings (P/E), price-to-book (P/B), and price-to-sales (P/S) ratios.

These metrics can help you identify stocks that may be trading at a discount compared to their historical averages or their industry peers.However, low valuation ratios alone do not necessarily indicate an undervalued stock. It's essential to dig deeper into the company's fundamentals, such as its competitive position, growth prospects, and management quality. Look for companies with strong competitive advantages, such as a dominant market share, proprietary technology, or a well-recognized brand. These companies may be able to maintain their profitability and growth even in challenging market conditions.Another factor to consider when identifying undervalued stocks is the company's growth potential. Look for companies with a track record of consistent revenue and earnings growth, as well as a clear path for future growth. This may include new product launches, expansion into new markets, or successful execution of strategic initiatives.When analyzing ETFs for potential undervaluation, focus on the underlying index or investment theme. Look for ETFs that track well-established and diversified indices, such as the S&P 500 or the MSCI EAFE, which have historically generated strong returns over the long term. Also, consider the expense ratio of the ETF, as higher fees can eat into your returns and make the ETF less attractive compared to its peers.Remember that identifying undervalued stocks and ETFs is an art, not a science. Market sentiment, economic conditions, and unexpected events can all impact the valuation of securities. It's essential to maintain a long-term perspective and diversify your investments to mitigate the risks associated with individual stock or ETF selections.

6. Dollar-Cost Averaging and Regular Investing

Dollar-cost averaging involves investing a fixed amount of money at regular intervals, regardless of market conditions, to reduce the impact of market volatility on your investment returns. Implementing a dollar-cost averaging strategy with regular investments in stocks and ETFs can help smooth out market fluctuations and build wealth over time through disciplined and consistent investing.The key principle behind dollar-cost averaging is to invest a fixed amount of money at regular intervals, such as weekly, monthly, or quarterly. By doing so, you automatically buy more shares when prices are low and fewer shares when prices are high, effectively averaging out the cost of your investments over time.One of the main advantages of dollar-cost averaging is that it helps to reduce the impact of market volatility on your investment returns. By investing consistently, regardless of market conditions, you avoid the temptation to time the market, which can be a risky and often unsuccessful strategy. Dollar-cost averaging also helps to instill discipline in your investing habits, as you commit to investing a fixed amount at regular intervals. Another benefit of dollar-cost averaging is that it can help to build wealth over time through the power of compounding. By consistently investing a fixed amount, you can take advantage of the long-term growth potential of the stock market and compound your returns over time. This can be particularly effective when combined with a long-term investment horizon and a diversified portfolio of stocks and ETFs. To implement a dollar-cost averaging strategy, set up automatic transfers from your bank account to your investment account at regular intervals. Many brokerages and investment platforms offer automatic investment plans that allow you to set up recurring investments in specific stocks or ETFs. Stick to your plan and continue investing consistently, even during market downturns, as this can help you take advantage of lower prices and position your portfolio for long-term growth.

7. Minimizing Investment Fees and Taxes

Minimizing investment fees and taxes is essential for maximizing your investment returns and preserving capital. Choose low-cost brokerage accounts and investment platforms to reduce transaction costs and management fees associated with buying and selling stocks and ETFs. Consider tax-efficient investment strategies, such as holding investments in tax-advantaged accounts or utilizing tax-loss harvesting to minimize tax liabilities and optimize after-tax returns.Investment fees can have a significant impact on your long-term investment returns, as they compound over time. High fees can eat into your returns and make it more difficult to achieve your financial goals. When selecting a brokerage account or investment platform, look for low trading commissions, no account maintenance fees, and competitive expense ratios on any mutual funds or ETFs you may invest in.Tax-efficient investing is another important consideration when building your stock and ETF portfolio. Holding investments in tax-advantaged accounts, such as 401(k)s, IRAs, or Roth accounts, can help you defer or eliminate taxes on your investment earnings. Contributions to these accounts may also be tax-deductible, providing an additional boost to your investment returns. Tax-loss harvesting is another strategy that can help minimize your tax liabilities. This involves selling investments that have declined in value to offset capital gains from other investments or to claim a tax deduction. The proceeds from the sale can then be used to purchase a similar investment, maintaining your desired asset allocation while realizing a tax benefit. When investing in taxable accounts, consider the tax implications of your investment choices. Stocks that pay qualified dividends and ETFs that track broad market indices tend to be more tax-efficient than other types of investments. Consult with a tax professional or financial advisor to develop a tax-efficient investment strategy that aligns with your overall financial goals and risk tolerance.

8. Rebalancing Your Portfolio Regularly

Rebalancing your portfolio involves periodically adjusting your asset allocation to maintain your desired risk profile and investment objectives. Review your stock and ETF holdings regularly, and reallocate assets as needed to ensure that your portfolio remains diversified and aligned with your long-term investment strategy. Rebalancing can help manage risk, capture gains, and optimize returns over time. Over time, as some investments outperform others, your portfolio's asset allocation will naturally drift from your original targets. For example, if stocks have performed well, they may make up a larger portion of your portfolio than intended, increasing your overall risk exposure. Rebalancing involves selling some of the investments that have grown too large and using the proceeds to buy more of the investments that have become underweighted. The frequency of rebalancing can vary depending on your investment strategy and market conditions. Some investors choose to rebalance on a set schedule, such as annually or semi-annually, while others may rebalance when their asset allocation deviates from their target by a certain percentage. It's important to find a rebalancing strategy that works for you and stick to it consistently. Rebalancing can provide several benefits, including:

1. **Risk management**: Rebalancing helps to maintain your desired risk profile by ensuring that your portfolio is not overly exposed to any single asset class or sector.

2. **Capturing gains**: By selling investments that have appreciated in value, rebalancing allows you to capture gains and lock in profits.

3. **Optimizing returns**: Rebalancing can help you buy low and sell high, as you are selling investments that have become overvalued and buying those that have become undervalued.

4. **Maintaining discipline**: Rebalancing forces you to take a disciplined approach to investing, as it requires you to make tough decisions about selling investments that have performed well and buying those that have underperformed.

When rebalancing your portfolio, consider the tax implications of your actions. Selling investments in taxable accounts may trigger capital gains taxes, which can eat into your returns. Consult with a tax professional or financial advisor to develop a rebalancing strategy that minimizes your tax liabilities while maintaining your desired asset allocation.

9. Investing in Index Funds and ETFs for Passive Income

Investing in index funds and ETFs offers a passive and cost-effective way to gain exposure to broad market indices and diversified asset classes. Index funds and ETFs track the performance of benchmark indices, providing investors with instant diversification and low management fees. Consider incorporating index funds and ETFs into your investment portfolio to achieve broad market exposure and generate passive income over the long term.Index funds and ETFs offer several advantages over actively managed mutual funds:

1. **Lower fees**: Index funds and ETFs typically have lower expense ratios than actively managed funds, as they do not require a team of analysts and portfolio managers to select individual securities.

2. **Broad diversification**: By tracking a broad market index, index funds and ETFs provide instant diversification across multiple sectors and industries, reducing the impact of individual stock or sector performance on your portfolio.

3. **Tax efficiency**: Index funds and ETFs tend to be more tax-efficient than actively managed funds, as they have lower turnover and fewer capital gains distributions.

4. **Consistent performance**: Over the long term, index funds and ETFs have often outperformed actively managed funds, as they avoid the costs and risks associated with trying to beat the market.

When selecting index funds and ETFs, consider factors such as the underlying index, expense ratio, trading volume, and tracking error. Look for funds that track well-established indices, such as the S&P 500 or the MSCI EAFE, and have low expense ratios and minimal tracking error.Investing in index funds and ETFs can provide a solid foundation for your investment portfolio, offering broad market exposure and the potential for long-term growth. By allocating a portion of your portfolio to these passive investments, you can reduce your overall investment costs and simplify your investment management while still participating in the growth of the stock market.

10. Monitoring and Adjusting Your Stock and ETF Investments

Monitoring and adjusting your stock and ETF investments is essential for staying informed about market trends, economic developments, and changes in company fundamentals. Regularly review your investment portfolio, track performance metrics, and assess the impact of external factors on your investments. Stay proactive in adjusting your investment strategy based on new information, market conditions, and evolving financial goals to optimize your investment outcomes. When monitoring your stock and ETF investments, pay attention to key performance indicators such as total return, dividend yield, expense ratio, and volatility. Track the performance of individual securities and funds relative to their benchmarks and peer groups to evaluate their relative strength and weakness. Regularly review your asset allocation, sector exposure, and geographic diversification to ensure that your portfolio remains aligned with your long-term investment strategy. Adjusting your stock and ETF investments may be necessary in response to changing market conditions, economic outlook, or personal financial goals. Consider rebalancing your portfolio periodically to maintain your desired asset allocation and risk profile. Reallocate assets from overperforming investments to underperforming ones to restore your target allocation and capture potential gains. Stay informed about company news, earnings reports, and economic indicators that may impact your investments, and be prepared to make adjustments as needed. Continuously educating yourself about investing, staying informed about market trends, and seeking advice from financial professionals can help you make informed decisions and navigate the complexities of the stock and ETF markets. Regularly review your investment strategy, assess your risk tolerance, and adjust your portfolio as needed to stay on track towards achieving your financial goals. By monitoring and adjusting your stock and ETF investments proactively, you can optimize your investment performance and build a resilient and diversified portfolio for long-term wealth accumulation.

Chapter 8. Peer-to-Peer Lending

Peer-to-peer lending has emerged as a popular alternative investment option, allowing individuals to lend money directly to borrowers through online platforms. This chapter explores the intricacies of peer-to-peer lending, providing insights into key strategies and considerations for successful participation in this growing financial market.

1. Understanding the Basics of Peer-to-Peer Lending

Peer-to-peer lending, also known as P2P lending, enables individuals to lend money to borrowers without the need for traditional financial institutions like banks. P2P lending platforms connect lenders with borrowers, facilitating loan transactions and providing an alternative source of financing for individuals and small businesses. Lenders earn interest on their loans, while borrowers gain access to funding that may be more flexible and affordable than traditional bank loans.P2P lending platforms typically operate online, offering a user-friendly interface for lenders to browse loan listings, select borrowers, and invest in loan opportunities. The platforms handle the loan origination process, credit assessment, and loan servicing, making it convenient for both lenders and borrowers to participate in the lending marketplace. P2P lending has gained popularity for its potential to generate attractive returns and diversify investment portfolios beyond traditional asset classes like stocks and bonds.One of the key advantages of peer-to-peer lending is the ability to bypass traditional financial intermediaries and directly connect lenders with borrowers. This disintermediation can lead to lower costs for borrowers and potentially higher returns for lenders, as the platforms often have lower overhead expenses compared to traditional banks. Additionally, P2P lending platforms often use advanced algorithms and data analytics to assess borrower creditworthiness, which can lead to more efficient credit allocation and risk management.However, it's important to note that peer-to-peer lending also carries risks, such as the potential for loan defaults, platform failures, and regulatory changes. Lenders should carefully evaluate the risks associated with each loan opportunity and the overall P2P lending platform before investing. Diversification, risk management, and due diligence are crucial when participating in the peer-to-peer lending market.

2. Evaluating Lending Platforms and Their Track Records

When considering peer-to-peer lending as an investment option, it's essential to evaluate lending platforms and their track records to assess their credibility, transparency, and performance. Research different P2P lending platforms to understand their loan offerings, interest rates, fees, and borrower profiles. Look for platforms with a solid reputation, regulatory compliance, and a history of successful loan originations and repayments.Reviewing the track record of lending platforms can provide valuable insights into their reliability and risk management practices. Consider factors such as loan default rates, investor returns, and platform stability to gauge the platform's performance and suitability for your investment goals. Look for platforms that offer detailed loan performance data, investor protection mechanisms, and clear communication channels to support a positive and secure lending experience.One important aspect to consider when evaluating P2P lending platforms is their regulatory compliance and investor protection measures. Reputable platforms should be registered with the appropriate financial authorities and adhere to strict guidelines regarding borrower verification, loan underwriting, and investor disclosures. Look for platforms that offer investor protection features, such as loan diversification, reserve funds, or buyback guarantees, to mitigate the risks associated with loan defaults.Additionally, assess the platform's user experience, customer support, and overall transparency. A well-designed platform with clear and accessible information about loan opportunities, fees, and performance can help lenders make informed decisions and manage their investments effectively. Platforms that prioritize transparency and provide regular updates on loan performance and platform developments are more likely to foster trust and confidence among lenders.

3. Assessing Borrower Creditworthiness and Risk

Assessing borrower creditworthiness and risk is a critical aspect of peer-to-peer lending to minimize the potential for loan defaults and losses. P2P lending platforms typically assign credit grades or scores to borrowers based on their credit history, income, employment status, and debt-to-income ratio. Evaluate borrower profiles, loan purposes, and financial stability indicators to determine the level of risk associated with each loan opportunity.When assessing borrower creditworthiness, consider factors such as the borrower's credit score, payment history, debt levels, and income stability. Higher credit scores and lower debt-to-income ratios generally indicate lower risk, while lower credit scores and higher debt levels may suggest higher risk. However, it's important to note that credit scores alone do not provide a complete picture of a borrower's creditworthiness, and other factors, such as the purpose of the loan and the borrower's overall financial situation, should also be taken into account.Diversifying your lending portfolio across different borrower risk profiles can help mitigate the impact of individual loan defaults. Consider allocating a portion of your investment to lower-risk borrowers with higher credit scores and stable financial profiles, while also investing in higher-risk borrowers with lower credit scores but compelling loan purposes or extenuating circumstances. This balanced approach can help optimize your risk-adjusted returns while maintaining a well-diversified portfolio.It's important to note that even with thorough borrower assessment, loan defaults can still occur. Unexpected life events, such as job loss, medical emergencies, or economic downturns, can impact a borrower's ability to repay their loan. As a lender, it's crucial to factor in the potential for defaults when calculating your expected returns and to maintain a diversified portfolio to minimize the impact of any individual loan default on your overall investment performance.

4. Diversifying Your Peer-to-Peer Lending Portfolio

Diversifying your peer-to-peer lending portfolio is a key risk management strategy that involves spreading your investments across multiple loans to reduce exposure to any single borrower or loan. By diversifying across different credit grades, loan terms, and borrower profiles, you can mitigate the impact of individual loan defaults and enhance the overall stability of your lending portfolio. Consider setting limits on the amount of capital you allocate to each loan to maintain a well-diversified and balanced portfolio.Diversification in peer-to-peer lending can take several forms. First, consider diversifying across different credit grades, allocating a portion of your investment to lower-risk borrowers with higher credit scores and another portion to higher-risk borrowers with lower credit scores but potentially higher returns. This approach can help balance your risk exposure while still allowing for potential upside.Second, diversify across loan terms, investing in a mix of short-term and long-term loans. Short-term loans, typically ranging from 6 to 36 months, can provide quicker access to your invested capital, while long-term loans, with terms of 3 to 5 years, may offer higher interest rates. By investing in a mix of loan terms, you can create a more balanced portfolio with varying cash flow and reinvestment needs.Third, diversify across different borrower profiles and loan purposes. Consider investing in a mix of personal loans, small business loans, and specialty loans, such as auto loans or student loan refinancing. Each loan type may have different risk profiles and potential returns, so diversifying across these categories can help reduce overall portfolio risk.Finally, consider setting investment limits on the amount of capital you allocate to each individual loan or borrower. Many P2P lending platforms recommend limiting your investment in any single loan to 1% or less of your total portfolio. This helps ensure that no single loan default has an outsized impact on your overall investment performance.By implementing a diversified approach to peer-to-peer lending, you can reduce the impact of individual loan defaults, smooth out returns over time, and create a more resilient investment portfolio. However, it's important to note that diversification alone does not guarantee against losses, and it's still crucial to carefully evaluate each loan opportunity and the overall P2P lending platform before investing.

5. Calculating Potential Returns and Risks

Calculating potential returns and risks in peer-to-peer lending involves analyzing the expected interest income, default rates, and platform fees associated with your loan investments. Use online calculators, investment tools, and historical performance data to estimate your projected returns and assess the level of risk you are comfortable with. Consider factors such as loan term, interest rate, loan purpose, and borrower creditworthiness when evaluating the risk-return profile of each loan opportunity.When calculating potential returns, start by considering the interest rate offered on each loan. P2P lending platforms typically offer a range of interest rates based on the borrower's credit profile and risk grade. Higher-risk borrowers may be offered higher interest rates, but this also comes with a higher probability of default. Lower-risk borrowers may have lower interest rates, but their loans are less likely to default.Next, factor in the potential for loan defaults and losses. While P2P lending platforms typically have robust credit assessment and risk management processes, some level of defaults is inevitable. Historical default rates for the platform and the specific loan grade can provide a starting point for estimating potential losses. However, it's important to note that past performance is not a guarantee of future results, and economic conditions can significantly impact default rates.Finally, consider the platform fees associated with your investment. P2P lending platforms typically charge origination fees when a loan is issued and may also charge servicing fees throughout the life of the loan. These fees can eat into your potential returns, so it's important to factor them into your calculations. Some platforms may also charge early withdrawal fees or other miscellaneous fees, so be sure to review the platform's fee structure carefully.By combining the expected interest income, potential default rates, and platform fees, you can estimate your projected returns for each loan opportunity. However, it's important to remember that these are estimates and that actual returns may vary based on a variety of factors, including economic conditions, borrower behavior, and platform performance.

6. Automating Your Lending Process for Passive Income

Automating your lending process for passive income involves setting up automatic investments, reinvesting returns, and leveraging auto-invest tools provided by P2P lending platforms. By automating your lending activities, you can save time, reduce manual effort, and ensure that your funds are continuously invested in new loan opportunities. Reinvesting your returns can help compound your earnings over time and maximize the growth potential of your peer-to-peer lending portfolio.One of the key benefits of automating your peer-to-peer lending process is the ability to invest consistently and efficiently. By setting up automatic investments, you can allocate a fixed amount of capital to new loan opportunities on a regular basis, such as weekly or monthly. This helps ensure that your funds are continuously deployed and earning interest, rather than sitting idle in your account.Many P2P lending platforms offer auto-invest tools that allow you to set specific criteria for loan selection, such as credit grade, loan term, and interest rate. These tools can automatically allocate your funds to loans that meet your specified criteria, saving you time and effort in manually selecting each loan opportunity. Some platforms even offer automated portfolio rebalancing, which can help maintain your desired risk profile and asset allocation over time.Reinvesting your returns is another powerful strategy for maximizing the growth potential of your peer-to-peer lending portfolio. Instead of withdrawing your interest earnings, consider automatically reinvesting them in new loan opportunities. This allows your returns to compound over time, as the interest earned on your reinvested funds generates additional interest, and so on. Over the long run, this compounding effect can significantly boost your overall investment returns.However, it's important to note that automating your lending process does not eliminate the need for due diligence and risk management. It's still crucial to carefully evaluate the P2P lending platform, the loan opportunities, and the potential risks before investing. Automating your process can help streamline your investments, but it should not replace your own analysis and decision-making.

7. Monitoring and Managing Your Peer-to-Peer Lending Investments

Monitoring and managing your peer-to-peer lending investments is essential for staying informed about loan performance, borrower updates, and platform developments. Regularly review your loan portfolio, track repayment schedules, and assess the impact of late payments or defaults on your investment returns. Stay proactive in managing your lending activities, adjusting your investment strategy as needed, and staying informed about market trends and regulatory changes that may impact your P2P lending investments.One of the key aspects of monitoring your peer-to-peer lending investments is tracking the performance of individual loans and your overall portfolio. Most P2P lending platforms provide detailed reporting on loan status, repayment history, and any late payments or defaults. Review this information regularly to stay informed about the performance of your investments and identify any potential issues early on.If you notice a borrower is late on a payment or appears to be experiencing financial difficulties, it's important to communicate with them proactively. Many platforms provide tools for lenders to communicate with borrowers and offer assistance in resolving payment issues. By working with the borrower and the platform, you may be able to find a solution that allows the loan to continue performing, such as a temporary payment plan or a loan modification.In the event of a loan default, the P2P lending platform will typically initiate collection efforts on behalf of lenders. However, it's still important to stay informed about the status of the defaulted loan and any recovery efforts. Some platforms may offer lenders the option to sell their portion of a defaulted loan to other investors, providing a potential avenue for recovering some of the invested capital.Regularly reviewing your overall investment strategy and making adjustments as needed is also crucial for managing your peer-to-peer lending portfolio effectively. As your financial goals, risk tolerance, or market conditions change, you may need to rebalance your portfolio, adjust your investment criteria, or allocate capital to different loan opportunities or platforms. Stay informed about industry trends, regulatory changes, and platform developments that may impact your investments and be prepared to adapt your strategy accordingly.

8. Dealing with Late Payments and Defaults

Dealing with late payments and defaults is a common challenge in peer-to-peer lending that requires a proactive and strategic approach. Stay informed about borrower payment behavior, communicate with borrowers to address issues early, and work with the lending platform to resolve delinquencies and defaults. Consider diversifying your lending portfolio, setting aside reserves for potential losses, and adjusting your investment strategy to mitigate the impact of late payments and defaults on your overall returns.Late payments and defaults are an inevitable part of the peer-to-peer lending landscape, even with thorough borrower assessment and risk management practices. Unexpected life events, such as job loss, medical emergencies, or economic downturns, can impact a borrower's ability to repay their loan. As a lender, it's crucial to be prepared for the possibility of late payments and defaults and to have a plan in place for dealing with them effectively.One of the most important steps in dealing with late payments and defaults is to stay informed about borrower payment behavior and to communicate with borrowers proactively. Many P2P lending platforms provide tools for lenders to monitor loan performance and to reach out to borrowers who are behind on payments. By communicating with borrowers early and offering assistance, you may be able to help them get back on track with their payments and avoid default.If a borrower does default on their loan, the P2P lending platform will typically initiate collection efforts on behalf of lenders. The platform may offer lenders the option to sell their portion of the defaulted loan to other investors, providing a potential avenue for recovering some of the invested capital. However, it's important to note that the recovery process can be lengthy and may not always result in a full recovery of the invested funds.To mitigate the impact of late payments and defaults on your overall returns, consider diversifying your lending portfolio across different credit grades, loan terms, and borrower profiles.

By spreading your investments across a larger number of loans, you can reduce the impact of any single loan default on your overall portfolio performance. Additionally, consider setting aside reserves for potential losses, either by allocating a portion of your investment capital to a reserve fund or by factoring in an expected loss rate when calculating your potential returns.Finally, be prepared to adjust your investment strategy as needed in response to changing market conditions and borrower behavior. If you notice an increase in late payments or defaults, consider adjusting your investment criteria to focus on lower-risk borrowers or shorter-term loans. Stay informed about industry trends and regulatory changes that may impact the peer-to-peer lending market and be prepared to adapt your strategy accordingly.

9. Reinvesting Returns for Compounding Growth

Reinvesting returns for compounding growth is a key strategy in peer-to-peer lending to maximize the long-term growth potential of your investment portfolio. Instead of withdrawing your earnings, consider reinvesting them in new loan opportunities to generate additional interest income and accelerate the growth of your lending portfolio. Reinvesting returns can help compound your earnings over time, increase the size of your investment portfolio, and enhance the overall performance of your peer-to-peer lending investments.The power of compounding is a key advantage of reinvesting your returns in peer-to-peer lending. By reinvesting your interest earnings in new loan opportunities, you can generate additional interest on those reinvested funds, which in turn generates more interest, and so on. Over time, this compounding effect can significantly boost your overall investment returns.Many P2P lending platforms make it easy to reinvest your returns by offering automatic reinvestment features. These tools allow you to automatically allocate your interest earnings to new loan opportunities, ensuring that your funds are continuously deployed and earning interest. Some platforms may even offer enhanced returns or bonuses for lenders who choose to reinvest their earnings.When reinvesting your returns, it's important to maintain a diversified approach and to continue evaluating each loan opportunity based on its individual merits. Avoid the temptation to simply invest in the highest-yielding loans without considering the underlying risk. Instead, use your reinvestment strategy as an opportunity to further diversify your portfolio and to potentially adjust your risk profile over time.

10. Peer-to-Peer Lending as a Fixed-Income Investment Strategy

Peer-to-peer lending can be a fixed-income investment strategy that offers predictable cash flows, regular interest payments, and potential capital appreciation. By investing in loans with fixed interest rates and scheduled repayment terms, you can generate a steady stream of income and build a diversified portfolio of fixed-income assets. Consider peer-to-peer lending as a complement to other investment strategies, such as stocks and bonds, to achieve a balanced and resilient investment portfolio that aligns with your financial goals and risk tolerance.One of the key advantages of using peer-to-peer lending as a fixed-income investment strategy is the potential for higher returns compared to traditional fixed-income assets like bonds or CDs. P2P lending platforms often offer interest rates that are higher than those available from banks or the bond market, providing an opportunity for lenders to generate attractive yields on their investments.Additionally, peer-to-peer lending can provide diversification benefits to a fixed-income portfolio. By investing in a pool of loans with varying credit profiles and risk levels, lenders can potentially reduce their overall portfolio risk and smooth out returns over time. This diversification can help mitigate the impact of individual loan defaults and provide a more stable income stream compared to investing in a single fixed-income asset. When using peer-to-peer lending as a fixed-income strategy, it's important to carefully consider the risk profile of your investments and to maintain a well-diversified portfolio. While P2P lending can offer higher yields than traditional fixed-income assets, it also carries higher risk, particularly in the form of potential loan defaults. Lenders should carefully evaluate the creditworthiness of borrowers, the track record of the lending platform, and their own risk tolerance before allocating a significant portion of their fixed-income portfolio to P2P lending. Additionally, lenders should be aware of the potential liquidity constraints associated with peer-to-peer lending. Unlike bonds or CDs, which can be sold on a secondary market, P2P loans are typically held to maturity, which can limit the lender's ability to access their invested capital in the event of an emergency or a change in investment strategy. Lenders should carefully consider their liquidity needs and investment horizon when allocating capital to P2P lending as part of their fixed-income strategy. Overall, peer-to-peer lending can be a valuable addition to a fixed-income investment strategy, offering the potential for higher yields and diversification benefits.

However, lenders should carefully evaluate the risks associated with P2P lending and maintain a well-diversified portfolio that aligns with their overall investment objectives and risk tolerance.

Chapter 9. Automating and Scaling Your Passive Income

In the pursuit of building sustainable passive income streams, leveraging automation and scaling strategies can significantly enhance efficiency and growth. This chapter delves into key tactics and considerations for automating and scaling passive income businesses to maximize returns and long-term success.

1. Leveraging Technology to Automate Income Streams

Utilizing technology to automate income streams is a fundamental strategy for streamlining operations and freeing up time for strategic growth. Automation tools such as payment processors, customer relationship management (CRM) systems, and project management software can help automate repetitive tasks, streamline workflows, and improve overall productivity. By integrating technology solutions into your passive income business, you can reduce manual effort, increase efficiency, and focus on high-impact activities that drive revenue and growth. When selecting automation tools, prioritize solutions that seamlessly integrate with your existing systems and processes. Look for platforms that offer user-friendly interfaces, robust features, and reliable customer support. Automation tools can help streamline various aspects of your passive income business, such as:

1. **Payment processing**: Automate invoicing, recurring billing, and payment collection to ensure timely and accurate transactions.

2. **Lead management**: Utilize CRM systems to capture, nurture, and track leads, ensuring efficient sales and customer relationship management.

3. **Content management**: Leverage content management systems (CMS) to create, publish, and optimize content for your passive income streams.

4. **Task scheduling**: Automate task assignments, deadlines, and progress tracking to ensure timely completion of projects and deliverables.

By implementing automation tools strategically, you can reduce manual errors, improve data accuracy, and free up valuable time for higher-level tasks that drive business growth and profitability.

2. Outsourcing and Delegating Tasks to Virtual Assistants

Outsourcing and delegating tasks to virtual assistants can help offload non-core activities, free up valuable time, and scale your passive income business effectively. Virtual assistants can handle administrative tasks, customer support, content creation, and other operational responsibilities, allowing you to focus on strategic decision-making and business development. By leveraging virtual assistants, you can optimize resource allocation, improve operational efficiency, and accelerate business growth without the need for significant overhead costs.When outsourcing tasks to virtual assistants, it's essential to establish clear communication channels, set expectations, and provide detailed instructions. Invest time in training and onboarding virtual assistants to ensure they understand your business objectives, processes, and standards. Regular check-ins and performance reviews can help maintain quality and identify areas for improvement.Some key tasks that can be effectively outsourced to virtual assistants include:

1. **Email management**: Handle inbox organization, email responses, and customer inquiries.

2. **Social media management**: Create and schedule social media posts, engage with followers, and monitor brand mentions.

3. **Content creation**: Assist with research, writing, editing, and formatting of blog posts, articles, and other content assets.

4. **Data entry and analysis**: Input data, maintain spreadsheets, and generate reports for informed decision-making.

5. **Customer support**: Provide first-line support, answer FAQs, and escalate complex issues to the appropriate team members.

By carefully selecting and managing virtual assistants, you can scale your passive income business without sacrificing quality or customer satisfaction.

3. Scaling Your Passive Income Business Through Partnerships

Scaling your passive income business through partnerships can unlock new growth opportunities, expand your reach, and diversify your income streams. Collaborating with complementary businesses, influencers, or industry experts can help you tap into new markets, access new customer segments, and leverage existing networks for mutual benefit. Strategic partnerships can also provide access to specialized expertise, resources, and distribution channels that can accelerate the growth of your passive income business.When exploring partnership opportunities, focus on aligning with businesses or individuals that share your values, target audience, and growth objectives. Conduct thorough research to assess the potential partner's reputation, credibility, and compatibility with your brand. Establish clear communication channels, define roles and responsibilities, and create a mutually beneficial agreement that outlines the terms of the partnership.Some effective partnership strategies for scaling your passive income business include:

1. **Affiliate marketing**: Collaborate with affiliates or influencers to promote your products or services in exchange for a commission on sales.

2. **Co-branding**: Partner with a complementary brand to create co-branded products, services, or content that appeals to a wider audience.

3. **Joint ventures**: Collaborate with another business to develop and market a new

product or service, sharing resources, risks, and rewards.

4. **Referral programs**: Incentivize existing customers or partners to refer new customers to your business, driving growth through word-of-mouth marketing.

5. **White-label partnerships**: Provide your products or services to other businesses under their own brand, leveraging their existing customer base and distribution channels.

By carefully selecting and managing strategic partnerships, you can accelerate the growth of your passive income business while minimizing risk and maximizing returns.

4. Automating Content Creation and Marketing

Automating content creation and marketing processes can help you consistently deliver high-quality content, engage your audience, and drive traffic to your passive income streams. Utilize content management systems, social media scheduling tools, and email marketing automation platforms to streamline content creation, distribution, and promotion. By automating these processes, you can maintain a consistent online presence, attract new customers, and nurture existing relationships without constant manual intervention. When automating content creation and marketing, focus on creating a content strategy that aligns with your business objectives and target audience. Develop a content calendar that outlines the topics, formats, and distribution channels for your content assets. Leverage content management systems to streamline the content creation process, enabling multiple team members to collaborate on content development and publication. Social media scheduling tools can help you maintain a consistent presence across various platforms by allowing you to pre-schedule posts, monitor engagement, and analyze performance metrics. Automation can also help you respond to comments, engage with followers, and participate in relevant conversations, fostering a sense of community around your brand. Email marketing automation platforms enable you to create targeted campaigns, segment your audience, and deliver personalized content based on user behavior and preferences. Automated email sequences can nurture leads, promote products or services, and re-engage inactive subscribers, driving conversions and revenue growth. By automating content creation and marketing processes, you can ensure that your passive income business maintains a strong online presence, delivers value to your audience consistently, and generates a steady stream of leads and sales. However, it's essential to balance automation with human oversight to maintain the authenticity and relevance of your content and marketing efforts.

5. Using Email Marketing and Automation for Passive Income

Email marketing and automation are powerful tools for nurturing leads, converting prospects, and generating passive income. Implement email marketing campaigns, automated drip sequences, and personalized content to engage your audience, promote your products or services, and drive conversions. By leveraging email marketing automation, you can deliver targeted messages, track customer interactions, and optimize your campaigns for maximum impact and revenue generation.When using email marketing and automation for passive income, focus on building a high-quality email list of engaged subscribers. Offer valuable lead magnets, such as ebooks, webinars, or exclusive content, to incentivize email sign-ups. Segment your list based on user behavior, interests, and demographics to deliver personalized content that resonates with each subscriber.Automated email sequences can help nurture leads and guide them through the sales funnel. Create a series of emails that introduce your brand, educate your audience, and gradually promote your products or services. Trigger these sequences based on specific user actions, such as downloading a lead magnet, abandoning a shopping cart, or expressing interest in a particular product.Personalization is key to effective email marketing. Utilize dynamic content, personalized subject lines, and targeted recommendations to make each subscriber feel valued and engaged. Analyze email performance metrics, such as open rates, click-through rates, and conversion rates, to optimize your campaigns and improve their effectiveness over time.Integrating email marketing with your passive income streams can help drive consistent revenue growth. Promote your products or services through email campaigns, offer exclusive discounts or bonuses to subscribers, and cross-sell or upsell related products to increase customer lifetime value.By leveraging email marketing and automation, you can nurture leads, build customer loyalty, and generate passive income without the need for constant manual intervention. However, it's essential to maintain a balance between automation and personalization, ensuring that your email campaigns feel authentic and valuable to your subscribers.

6. Leveraging Social Media and Influencer Marketing

Social media and influencer marketing can be effective channels for expanding your passive income streams, reaching new audiences, and driving engagement. Develop a social media strategy, create compelling content, and collaborate with influencers or brand ambassadors to amplify your message and increase brand awareness. By leveraging social media platforms and influencer partnerships, you can enhance your online presence, build credibility, and attract a loyal following that can translate into passive income opportunities.When developing your social media strategy, focus on the platforms that align with your target audience and business objectives. Maintain an active presence on these platforms by consistently creating and sharing valuable content, engaging with your followers, and participating in relevant conversations. Utilize social media scheduling tools to streamline content creation and distribution, ensuring a consistent online presence without the need for constant manual effort.Influencer marketing can help you tap into new audiences and leverage the trust and credibility of established personalities in your industry. Collaborate with influencers whose values, audience, and content align with your brand. Negotiate mutually beneficial partnerships, such as sponsored content, affiliate marketing, or co-created content, to maximize the impact of your influencer marketing efforts.Measure the performance of your social media and influencer marketing campaigns using analytics tools. Track metrics such as reach, engagement, website traffic, and conversions to assess the effectiveness of your efforts and optimize your strategy accordingly. Continuously experiment with different content formats, posting schedules, and influencer partnerships to identify the most effective approaches for your passive income business.By leveraging social media and influencer marketing, you can build brand awareness, attract new customers, and drive traffic to your passive income streams. However, it's essential to maintain authenticity and transparency in your social media and influencer marketing efforts to preserve the trust and loyalty of your audience.

7. Optimizing Your Passive Income Streams for Maximum Returns

Optimizing your passive income streams involves continuously evaluating performance, identifying areas for improvement, and implementing strategies to maximize returns. Analyze key performance indicators, track revenue metrics, and conduct A/B testing to optimize your products, pricing, and marketing efforts. By regularly monitoring and optimizing your passive income streams, you can enhance profitability, drive growth, and ensure long-term sustainability in a competitive market landscape.When optimizing your passive income streams, start by defining your key performance indicators (KPIs) and revenue metrics. Depending on your business model, these may include conversion rates, average order value, customer lifetime value, or passive income growth rate. Regularly track and analyze these metrics to identify trends, patterns, and areas for improvement.A/B testing can help you optimize various aspects of your passive income streams, such as product descriptions, pricing, landing pages, and marketing messages. Create two versions of a specific element, split your audience, and compare the performance of each version to determine which one is more effective. Utilize A/B testing to continuously refine and improve your passive income offerings.Regularly review and update your pricing strategy to ensure that your products or services are competitively priced and aligned with market demand. Consider factors such as production costs, customer perceived value, and competitor pricing when setting your prices. Experiment with different pricing models, such as tiered pricing, bundling, or dynamic pricing, to optimize revenue and profitability.Continuously monitor and adapt your marketing efforts to ensure that you are effectively reaching and engaging your target audience. Analyze the performance of your various marketing channels, such as email, social media, or paid advertising, and allocate resources to the most effective channels. Experiment with new marketing tactics and strategies to stay ahead of the curve and maintain a competitive edge.By regularly optimizing your passive income streams, you can enhance profitability, drive growth, and ensure long-term sustainability in a competitive market landscape. However, it's essential to balance optimization efforts with maintaining the quality and authenticity of your products or services to preserve customer trust and loyalty.

8. Diversifying Your Passive Income Sources

Diversifying your passive income sources is a prudent strategy for reducing risk, increasing resilience, and maximizing revenue potential. Explore different income streams such as affiliate marketing, rental properties, digital products, and investments to create a diversified portfolio of passive income sources. By diversifying your income streams, you can mitigate the impact of market fluctuations, capitalize on multiple revenue streams, and build a more robust financial foundation for long-term wealth accumulation.When diversifying your passive income sources, consider factors such as your skills, interests, and risk tolerance. Leverage your existing knowledge and expertise to explore new passive income opportunities that align with your strengths and preferences. Conduct thorough research to assess the potential risks, returns, and scalability of each income stream before investing time and resources.Diversification can take many forms, such as:

1. **Investing in a mix of asset classes**: Allocate capital to a diverse portfolio of stocks, bonds, real estate, and alternative investments to reduce overall risk and enhance returns.

2. **Developing multiple digital products**: Create a suite of digital products, such as ebooks, online courses, or software applications, to appeal to a wider audience and generate multiple revenue streams.

3. **Engaging in multiple affiliate marketing partnerships**: Promote a variety of

products or services from different merchants to diversify your income sources and reduce reliance on a single merchant.

4. **Investing in multiple rental properties**: Build a portfolio of rental properties in different geographic locations and asset classes to mitigate the impact of local market fluctuations.

5. **Pursuing multiple passive income opportunities simultaneously**: Combine various passive income strategies, such as affiliate marketing, digital products, and investments, to create a diversified portfolio of income streams.

By diversifying your passive income sources, you can reduce the impact of individual failures or setbacks, smooth out income fluctuations, and create a more resilient and sustainable passive income portfolio. However, it's essential to maintain a balanced approach, allocating resources to each income stream based on its potential returns, risks, and scalability.

9. Scaling Your Passive Income Business While Maintaining Quality

Scaling your passive income business while maintaining quality requires a strategic approach that balances growth with customer satisfaction and operational excellence. Focus on scalability, efficiency, and automation to handle increased demand without compromising on product quality or customer experience. Invest in infrastructure, technology, and talent to support growth, optimize processes, and deliver consistent value to your audience. By prioritizing quality while scaling your passive income business, you can sustain long-term success and build a loyal customer base that drives sustainable revenue growth.When scaling your passive income business, prioritize the development of scalable systems and processes. Identify bottlenecks, streamline workflows, and automate repetitive tasks to ensure that your business can handle increased demand without sacrificing quality or efficiency. Invest in robust infrastructure, such as reliable hosting, secure payment processing, and scalable content management systems, to support growth and maintain a seamless customer experience.Leverage technology to automate and optimize various aspects of your business, such as customer support, content creation, and marketing. Utilize tools and platforms that enable you to handle increased volume without the need for significant manual intervention. Continuously monitor and optimize these systems to ensure that they remain efficient, effective, and aligned with your growth objectives.As your passive income business scales, it's essential to maintain a strong focus on quality and customer satisfaction. Regularly gather customer feedback, monitor performance metrics, and identify areas for improvement. Invest in talent and resources to support growth, such as hiring skilled team members or outsourcing tasks to virtual assistants. Ensure that your products or services consistently deliver value to your customers and maintain a high level of quality as your business scales.Building a loyal customer base is crucial for sustaining long-term growth and profitability. Focus on delivering exceptional customer experiences, providing responsive support, and fostering a sense of community around your brand. Encourage customer feedback, address concerns promptly, and continuously improve your offerings based on customer needs and preferences. By prioritizing quality and customer satisfaction while scaling your passive income business, you can build a strong foundation for sustainable growth and success.

10. Continuously Learning and Adapting to New Opportunities

Continuously learning and adapting to new opportunities is essential for staying competitive, innovative, and resilient in the ever-evolving landscape of passive income. Stay informed about industry trends, emerging technologies, and market developments to identify new revenue streams, optimize existing strategies, and capitalize on growth opportunities. Embrace a growth mindset, seek out learning opportunities, and be open to experimentation and adaptation to stay ahead of the curve and maximize the potential of your passive income ventures.In today's fast-paced business environment, the ability to adapt and learn is a critical success factor for passive income entrepreneurs. Regularly engage in professional development activities, such as attending industry conferences, participating in online courses, or joining relevant communities of practice. Seek out mentors or experts who can provide guidance, feedback, and insights to help you navigate the challenges and opportunities of building passive income streams.Embrace a culture of continuous improvement and innovation within your passive income business. Encourage team members to share ideas, experiment with new approaches, and learn from failures. Allocate resources to research and development, exploring emerging technologies, business models, and market trends that could impact your passive income streams. Be open to pivoting or adapting your strategies as needed to capitalize on new opportunities or mitigate emerging risks.Regularly review and update your passive income strategies based on changing market conditions, customer preferences, and technological advancements. Continuously monitor industry trends, analyze competitor moves, and gather customer feedback to inform your decision-making. Adapt your products, pricing, marketing, and operations as needed to stay relevant and competitive in a rapidly evolving landscape.Cultivate a growth mindset within your organization, embracing challenges as opportunities for learning and improvement. Encourage team members to step out of their comfort zones, take calculated risks, and embrace new experiences. Celebrate failures as learning opportunities and use them to inform future decisions and strategies.By continuously learning and adapting to new opportunities, you can position your passive income business for long-term success and growth. Stay curious, embrace change, and be willing to experiment and innovate to capitalize on emerging trends and market shifts. With a commitment to lifelong learning and adaptation, you can build a resilient and sustainable passive income portfolio that generates consistent returns and creates value for your customers over the long term.

Chapter 10. Maintaining and Optimizing Your Passive Income

Building and sustaining passive income streams requires ongoing maintenance, optimization, and a long-term perspective. This final chapter explores key strategies and considerations for maintaining and optimizing your passive income over time, ensuring its continued growth and resilience.

1. Monitoring and Analyzing Your Passive Income Streams

Regularly monitoring and analyzing your passive income streams is essential for identifying areas for improvement, optimizing performance, and making informed decisions. Track key metrics such as revenue, growth rates, customer engagement, and profitability to assess the health and performance of each income stream. Utilize data analytics tools and dashboards to gather insights and identify trends that can inform your optimization efforts.Monitoring your passive income streams involves tracking various performance indicators, such as revenue, expenses, customer engagement, and market trends. By regularly analyzing these metrics, you can identify opportunities for growth, detect potential issues early, and make data-driven decisions to optimize your passive income streams effectively.Revenue tracking is crucial for understanding the performance of your income sources. Monitor your income streams to identify which ones are performing well and which may need attention. Analyze revenue trends over time to spot patterns, seasonal fluctuations, or sudden changes that may require further investigation or action.Expense tracking is equally important for ensuring that your passive income remains profitable. Keep a close eye on your costs, including platform fees, advertising expenses, content creation costs, and any other associated expenses. Identify areas where you can reduce costs without compromising quality or performance, and allocate those savings towards growth initiatives or reinvestment.Customer engagement metrics provide valuable insights into how your audience interacts with your products or services. Analyze customer feedback, reviews, and support inquiries to identify areas for improvement or opportunities to enhance the customer experience. Track engagement metrics such as website traffic, email open rates, and social media interactions to gauge the effectiveness of your marketing efforts and identify opportunities to better connect with your target audience.Market trend analysis helps you stay informed about industry developments, competitor activities, and external factors that may impact your passive income streams. Monitor industry publications, attend conferences, and engage with your professional network to stay abreast of emerging trends, best practices, and potential threats. Adjust your strategies as needed to adapt to changing market conditions and maintain a competitive edge.By regularly monitoring and analyzing these key metrics, you can gain valuable insights into the performance and health of your passive income streams. Use this data to inform your decision-making, optimize your strategies, and ensure the long-term sustainability and growth of your passive income portfolio.

2. Identifying Areas for Improvement and Optimization

Based on your analysis, identify areas within your passive income streams that have room for improvement or optimization. This could include enhancing product quality, improving customer experience, optimizing marketing strategies, or streamlining operational processes. Prioritize areas that have the greatest potential for impact and allocate resources accordingly.Areas for improvement and optimization may include product or service quality, customer experience, marketing strategies, and operational efficiency. By focusing on continuous improvement and optimization, you can enhance the performance and profitability of your passive income streams, ensuring long-term success and sustainability.Product or service quality is a critical area for optimization. Regularly assess your offerings to ensure they continue to meet the evolving needs and expectations of your customers. Gather customer feedback, monitor industry trends, and stay up-to-date with technological advancements to identify opportunities for product enhancements or new feature development. Invest in research and development to create innovative products that set you apart from competitors and drive customer loyalty.Customer experience optimization is another key focus area. Streamline the purchasing process, improve customer support, and enhance user satisfaction to drive loyalty and retention. Analyze customer touchpoints, identify pain points, and implement strategies to create a seamless and enjoyable experience for your audience. Utilize customer feedback, user testing, and data analytics to continuously refine and improve the customer journey.Marketing strategy optimization can significantly impact the reach and effectiveness of your passive income streams.

Refine your messaging, targeting, and channels to engage your audience more effectively. Experiment with different marketing tactics, such as content marketing, social media advertising, or influencer partnerships, to identify the most effective approaches for your specific audience and business model. Continuously test and iterate your marketing strategies based on performance data and customer insights.Operational efficiency is crucial for maintaining profitability and scalability. Identify bottlenecks, automate repetitive tasks, and streamline workflows to increase productivity and reduce costs. Leverage technology solutions, such as project management tools, content management systems, and customer relationship management (CRM) platforms, to optimize your operations and free up time for strategic initiatives. Regularly review and refine your processes to ensure they remain efficient and aligned with your business goals.By prioritizing areas for improvement and optimization, you can make targeted investments that yield the greatest returns for your passive income streams. Allocate resources to the areas with the highest potential impact, and continuously monitor and adjust your optimization efforts to maintain a competitive edge and drive sustainable growth.

3. Reinvesting Profits and Compounding Wealth

Reinvesting a portion of your passive income profits back into your business can help accelerate growth, expand your offerings, and compound your wealth over time. Consider allocating funds towards developing new products, enhancing existing ones, or exploring new passive income opportunities. Reinvesting profits strategically can create a virtuous cycle of growth and wealth accumulation.Strategies for reinvesting profits and compounding wealth include product development, marketing initiatives, technology upgrades, and diversification. By reinvesting profits wisely and compounding your wealth over time, you can build a stronger and more resilient passive income portfolio that generates sustainable returns and long-term wealth accumulation.Product development is a key area for reinvestment, as it allows you to create new revenue streams and stay ahead of market trends. Invest in research and development to identify emerging customer needs, industry shifts, and opportunities for innovation. Allocate funds towards creating new products or services that complement your existing offerings and appeal to a broader audience. By continuously expanding your product portfolio, you can drive growth, increase customer lifetime value, and generate multiple streams of passive income.Marketing initiatives are another important area for reinvestment. Allocate funds towards advertising, promotions, and branding efforts to expand your reach and attract new customers. Experiment with different marketing channels, such as social media, email marketing, or influencer partnerships, to identify the most effective approaches for your target audience. Invest in content creation, search engine optimization (SEO), and lead generation strategies to build brand awareness, drive traffic, and convert prospects into customers.Technology upgrades can significantly improve the efficiency, scalability, and customer experience of your passive income streams. Reinvest profits towards upgrading your infrastructure, tools, or systems to streamline operations, enhance security, and improve user experience. Invest in data analytics platforms, automation tools, and customer relationship management (CRM) systems to gain deeper insights, optimize processes, and deliver personalized experiences to your audience.Diversification is a powerful strategy for compounding wealth and reducing risk. Allocate a portion of your profits towards exploring new income streams, markets, or investment opportunities that align with your long-term goals and risk tolerance. Consider expanding into new product categories, targeting different customer segments, or investing in complementary businesses or assets. By diversifying your income sources, you can create a more resilient and balanced passive income portfolio that generates consistent returns and mitigates the impact of market fluctuations or industry changes. When reinvesting profits, it's essential to maintain a strategic and disciplined approach. Set clear goals, allocate resources based on potential impact and return on investment (ROI), and regularly monitor and adjust your reinvestment strategies based on performance data and market conditions. By reinvesting profits wisely and compounding your wealth over time, you can build a strong foundation for long-term financial security and independence.

4. Maintaining a Long-Term Perspective and Staying Disciplined

Building sustainable passive income requires a long-term perspective and disciplined approach. Avoid chasing short-term gains or get-rich-quick schemes, as they often lead to unsustainable practices and potential losses. Stay focused on your long-term goals, maintain consistent effort, and make decisions based on data and sound principles. Discipline and perseverance are key to weathering market fluctuations and achieving lasting success.Adopting a long-term perspective is crucial for building passive income streams that generate consistent returns over time. Resist the temptation to chase short-term gains or make decisions based on hype or speculation. Instead, focus on creating high-quality products, delivering exceptional customer experiences, and building a strong brand reputation. Understand that building sustainable passive income takes time, effort, and a commitment to continuous improvement and learning.Staying disciplined is essential for maintaining focus and consistency in your passive income efforts. Establish clear goals, create a structured plan of action, and stick to it even when faced with challenges or setbacks. Break down your long-term objectives into smaller, actionable steps, and celebrate milestones along the way. Maintain a consistent effort, allocating time and resources towards your passive income activities on a regular basis.Make decisions based on data and sound principles rather than emotions or impulses. Regularly review your performance metrics, gather customer feedback, and stay informed about industry trends and best practices. Use this information to guide your decision-making and optimize your strategies for long-term success. Avoid making hasty decisions or changes based on short-term fluctuations or external pressures.Discipline also extends to managing your finances and resources effectively. Allocate a portion of your passive income towards reinvestment, savings, and personal goals. Avoid overspending or making impulsive purchases that can derail your long-term financial stability. Maintain a balanced approach, ensuring that your passive income activities complement and support your overall financial well-being and life objectives.Perseverance is key to weathering market fluctuations, industry changes, and personal challenges that may arise during your passive income journey. Expect setbacks and be prepared to adapt and learn from them. Maintain a growth mindset, continuously seeking opportunities for improvement and innovation. Celebrate your successes, but also acknowledge the hard work and dedication that goes into building sustainable passive income streams.By maintaining a long-term perspective and staying disciplined, you can navigate the ups and downs of the passive income landscape and achieve lasting success. Embrace a patient and persistent approach, making decisions based on data and sound principles, and staying focused on your long-term goals. With discipline and perseverance, you can build a passive income portfolio that generates consistent returns and supports your financial independence and freedom.

5. Dealing with Setbacks and Challenges in Passive Income

Setbacks and challenges are inevitable when building passive income streams. Product failures, market shifts, or personal circumstances can disrupt your progress. Develop a resilient mindset and have contingency plans in place to mitigate risks and bounce back from setbacks. View challenges as opportunities for learning and growth, and use them to refine your strategies and become more adaptable.Setbacks and challenges are a natural part of the passive income journey, and how you respond to them can make all the difference in your long-term success. Product failures, for example, may occur due to changing customer preferences, technological advancements, or competitive pressures. Market shifts, such as economic downturns or industry disruptions, can impact the demand for your products or services. Personal circumstances, such as health issues, family emergencies, or unexpected life events, can also disrupt your passive income efforts.Developing a resilient mindset is crucial for navigating these challenges. Adopt a growth mindset, viewing setbacks as opportunities for learning and improvement rather than failures. Analyze what went wrong, identify lessons learned, and use this knowledge to refine your strategies and become more adaptable. Celebrate small wins, maintain a positive attitude, and stay focused on your long-term goals.Having contingency plans in place can help you mitigate risks and bounce back from setbacks more quickly. Diversify your income streams to reduce reliance on a single product or market. Maintain a cash reserve to cover unexpected expenses or temporary income disruptions. Develop backup plans for key aspects of your business, such as alternative suppliers, backup systems, or emergency support networks.When facing challenges, take a step back, assess the situation objectively, and develop a plan of action. Break down complex problems into smaller, manageable tasks, and tackle them one step at a time. Seek support from mentors, peers, or professionals who can provide guidance, advice, and a fresh perspective. Maintain open communication with your customers, partners, and stakeholders, keeping them informed about any changes or disruptions.Adapt your strategies as needed to address the challenges at hand. Be willing to pivot, experiment, and try new approaches if your current strategies are no longer effective. Continuously monitor the situation, gather feedback, and make adjustments to ensure your passive income streams remain resilient and adaptable in the face of changing circumstances.By developing a resilient mindset and having contingency plans in place, you can navigate setbacks and challenges more effectively. View these obstacles as opportunities for growth, learning, and improvement, and use them to refine your strategies and become a more adaptable and successful passive income entrepreneur.

6. Continuously Learning and Improving Your Skills

Continuously learning and improving your skills is essential for maintaining a competitive edge and adapting to changing market conditions. Engage in ongoing professional development, seek out mentors or experts, and stay informed about industry trends and best practices. Invest time and resources into enhancing your knowledge and skills, as they are the foundation for creating and optimizing successful passive income streams.In the rapidly evolving world of passive income, continuous learning is not just a nice-to-have, but a necessity for long-term success. The skills and strategies that work today may become obsolete tomorrow, as new technologies, platforms, and market trends emerge. By continuously learning and improving your skills, you can stay ahead of the curve, adapt to change, and maintain a competitive advantage.Engage in ongoing professional development activities to enhance your knowledge and skills. Attend industry conferences, workshops, or webinars to learn from experts, network with peers, and stay informed about the latest trends and best practices. Participate in online courses, certifications, or training programs to deepen your understanding of specific topics or tools relevant to your passive income business.Seek out mentors or experts who have achieved success in building passive income streams or related fields. Reach out to them for guidance, advice, and feedback on your strategies and plans. Attend their events, read their content, or engage with them directly to gain valuable insights and perspectives that can help you navigate challenges and accelerate your growth.Stay informed about industry trends, emerging technologies, and market developments that may impact your passive income streams. Follow industry publications, blogs, and social media accounts to stay up-to-date with the latest news and insights. Participate in online communities, forums, or groups to engage with other passive income entrepreneurs, share knowledge, and learn from each other's experiences.Invest time and resources into continuously improving your skills in areas such as product development, marketing, customer service, and business strategy. Identify areas where you can enhance your knowledge or capabilities, and create a learning plan to address those gaps. Allocate time for skill development, experiment with new approaches, and seek feedback to refine your abilities over time.By continuously learning and improving your skills, you can adapt to changing market conditions, identify new opportunities, and optimize your passive income streams for long-term success. Embrace a growth mindset, stay curious, and be willing to invest in your own professional development. The knowledge and skills you acquire will serve as the foundation for creating and sustaining successful passive income ventures throughout your entrepreneurial journey.

7. Balancing Passive Income with Personal and Professional Goals

While passive income can provide financial freedom and flexibility, it's essential to maintain a balanced approach that aligns with your personal and professional goals. Avoid becoming overly consumed by passive income pursuits at the expense of your health, relationships, or other important aspects of life. Set boundaries, prioritize self-care, and ensure that your passive income activities complement rather than detract from your overall well-being and life objectives.Building passive income streams can be an exciting and rewarding journey, but it's crucial to maintain a balanced approach that supports your overall well-being and life goals. Avoid becoming so consumed by your passive income pursuits that you neglect other important aspects of your life, such as your health, relationships, or personal growth.Set clear boundaries and priorities to ensure that your passive income activities align with your values and life objectives. Allocate time for self-care, leisure activities, and quality time with loved ones. Maintain a healthy work-life balance, taking breaks and vacations as needed to recharge and avoid burnout.Regularly assess whether your passive income activities are complementing or detracting from your overall well-being and life goals. If you find that your passive income pursuits are causing undue stress, neglecting important relationships, or preventing you from pursuing other meaningful activities, it may be time to reevaluate your approach.Consider the long-term impact of your passive income activities on your personal and professional goals. Will the financial freedom and flexibility provided by passive income enable you to pursue other aspirations, such as starting a family, traveling the world, or launching a passion project? Or will the demands of maintaining your passive income streams prevent you from achieving those goals? Maintain open communication with your loved ones about your passive income goals and the potential impact on your shared life objectives. Seek their support and understanding, and be willing to adjust your plans if necessary to ensure that your passive income activities complement rather than detract from your family's well-being and happiness.By maintaining a balanced approach to passive income, you can enjoy the benefits of financial freedom and flexibility while also prioritizing your personal and professional goals. Set boundaries, maintain a healthy lifestyle, and ensure that your passive income activities are aligned with your values and life objectives. With discipline and self-awareness, you can build a successful passive income portfolio while also nurturing the other important aspects of your life.

8. Achieving Financial Independence and Freedom

Building a diversified portfolio of passive income streams can help you achieve financial independence and freedom. As your passive income grows and compounds over time, it can eventually replace or exceed your active income, providing you with the flexibility to pursue your passions, spend more time with loved ones, or retire early. Financial independence is a powerful outcome of successful passive income strategies, enabling you to live life on your own terms.The ultimate goal of building passive income streams is to achieve financial independence and the freedom to live life on your own terms. As your passive income grows and compounds over time, it can eventually replace or exceed your active income, providing you with the flexibility to make choices that align with your values and aspirations.Financial independence means different things to different people. For some, it may mean having the option to retire early and pursue leisure activities or travel. For others, it may involve having the freedom to work on passion projects, start a business, or pursue creative endeavors without the pressure of relying on active income. Financial independence can also provide the means to spend more quality time with family, volunteer for causes you care about, or simply enjoy a more relaxed pace of life.Achieving financial independence through passive income requires a long-term commitment to building multiple income streams, reinvesting profits, and maintaining a disciplined approach. It's important to diversify your passive income sources across different platforms, products, and markets to mitigate risk and ensure stability. Continuously monitor and optimize your income streams, adapting to changing market conditions and emerging opportunities.As you approach financial independence, it's crucial to maintain a balanced approach that aligns with your personal and professional goals. Avoid becoming overly consumed by passive income pursuits at the expense of your health, relationships, or other important aspects of life. Set boundaries, prioritize self-care, and ensure that your passive income activities complement rather than detract from your overall well-being and life objectives.Celebrate your progress and milestones along the way, but also maintain a long-term perspective. Financial independence is not a destination, but a journey that requires ongoing maintenance, optimization, and adaptation. Stay committed to continuous learning, improvement, and innovation to ensure that your passive income streams remain resilient and adaptable in the face of changing circumstances.By achieving financial independence through passive income, you can unlock a world of possibilities and live life on your own terms. Pursue your passions, spend more time with loved ones, or simply enjoy the freedom to make choices that align with your values and aspirations. With discipline, perseverance, and a commitment to continuous improvement, you can build a successful passive income portfolio that supports your long-term financial well-being and personal fulfillment.

9. Giving Back and Using Passive Income for Good

Once you have achieved a level of financial stability and freedom through passive income, consider giving back and using your resources for positive impact. Support charitable causes, invest in social enterprises, or mentor aspiring entrepreneurs. Leverage your passive income to create meaningful change and make a difference in the lives of others. Giving back can be a deeply fulfilling aspect of your passive income journey, aligning your financial success with your values and making a lasting impact on the world around you.As you progress on your passive income journey and achieve financial stability and freedom, consider using your resources to make a positive impact on the world around you. Giving back can be a deeply fulfilling aspect of your entrepreneurial journey, aligning your financial success with your values and creating meaningful change in the lives of others.There are many ways to give back and use your passive income for good. Support charitable causes that align with your values, such as education, healthcare, poverty alleviation, or environmental conservation. Donate a portion of your profits to reputable non-profit organizations or crowdfunding campaigns that are making a tangible difference in their respective fields.Invest in social enterprises or mission-driven businesses that are using innovative approaches to tackle societal challenges. These organizations often combine the principles of business with a commitment to positive social and environmental impact. By investing in these enterprises, you can generate financial returns while also supporting the creation of a more equitable and sustainable world.Share your knowledge and experience with aspiring entrepreneurs by mentoring or coaching individuals who are just starting their passive income journeys. Offer guidance, advice, and support to help them navigate the challenges and opportunities of building successful online businesses. Participate in educational programs, workshops, or accelerators that provide resources and support to underserved communities or marginalized groups.Leverage your passive income to support causes that are important to you, whether it's funding scholarships, supporting medical research, or advocating for policy changes. Use your voice and influence to raise awareness about issues that matter to you and inspire others to take action. Collaborate with like-minded individuals or organizations to amplify your impact and create lasting change. Giving back can also take the form of volunteering your time and skills to support causes you care about. Offer pro bono services, participate in community projects, or volunteer with organizations that align with your values. By donating your time and expertise, you can make a tangible difference in the lives of others while also gaining personal fulfillment and a sense of purpose. As you build your passive income portfolio, consider allocating a portion of your profits towards giving back and making a positive impact. Align your philanthropic efforts with your values, skills, and resources to maximize your impact and create a lasting legacy. By using your passive income for good, you can inspire others, create meaningful change, and find deeper purpose in your entrepreneurial journey.

10. Inspiring Others and Sharing Your Passive Income Journey

As you progress on your passive income journey, consider sharing your experiences, insights, and lessons learned with others. Inspire and empower aspiring entrepreneurs by sharing your story, offering guidance, and providing a roadmap for building sustainable passive income streams. Your journey can serve as a source of motivation and hope for those seeking financial freedom and independence. By sharing your knowledge and experiences, you can pay it forward and contribute to the growth and success of the passive income community as a whole.As you build your passive income portfolio and achieve success, consider sharing your journey with others to inspire and empower aspiring entrepreneurs. Your story can serve as a source of motivation and hope for those seeking financial freedom and independence, providing a roadmap for building sustainable passive income streams.Share your experiences, both successes and failures, to provide a realistic and relatable perspective on the challenges and opportunities of building passive income. Offer guidance and advice based on the lessons you've learned along the way, helping others avoid common pitfalls and accelerate their own progress. Provide actionable tips and strategies that others can implement in their own passive income ventures, drawing from your own experiences and best practices.Leverage various platforms and channels to share your story and insights, such as blogs, podcasts, social media, or live events. Create content that is engaging, informative, and inspiring, using your unique voice and perspective to connect with your audience. Engage with your followers, respond to their questions and comments, and build a community around your passive income journey.Consider mentoring or coaching aspiring entrepreneurs directly, offering one-on-one guidance and support to help them navigate the challenges of building passive income streams. Share your knowledge, provide feedback on their ideas and strategies, and help them develop the skills and mindset necessary for success. By investing in the growth and development of others, you can pay it forward and contribute to the success of the passive income community as a whole.Inspire others by demonstrating the power of passive income to create financial freedom, flexibility, and positive impact. Share stories of how passive income has enabled you to pursue your passions, spend more time with loved ones, or make a difference in the world. Encourage others to dream big and take action towards their own financial goals and aspirations.By sharing your passive income journey, you can inspire and empower others to take control of their financial futures and create the life they desire. Your story can serve as a testament to the power of hard work, perseverance, and a commitment to continuous learning and improvement. By paying it forward and contributing to the growth and success of the passive income community, you can create a lasting legacy and make a positive impact on the world around you.

www.ingramcontent.com/pod-product-compliance
Lightning Source LLC
Chambersburg PA
CBHW050100230526
45470CB00004B/1607